BACKSTREET
A firsthand account of childhood in
a 1920s London slum

Written by Joyce Challis
Compiled and Edited by
Mike and Sue Challis

HEDDON PUBLISHING

First published in the United Kingdom in 2024
by Heddon Publishing

www.heddonpublishing.com

Copyright 2024 © Joyce Challis
c/o Susan Challis and Michael Challis (copyright holders)

The right of Joyce Challis to be identified as the author of this work has been asserted by the editors/copyright holders in accordance with the Copyright, Designs and Patents Act 1988.

Compiled and edited by Sue and Mike Challis

A catalogue record for this book is available from the British Library

ISBN 978-1-913166-88-5 (paperback)
978-1-913166-89-2 (ebook)

All rights reserved. No part of this publication may be reproduced, stored in a retrieval system or transmitted in any form or by any means, electric, mechanical, photocopying, recording or otherwise, without the prior permission of the publisher.

This publication is designed to provide accurate and authoritative information in regard to the subject matter covered. While the publisher and author have used their best efforts in preparing this book, they make no representations or warranties with respect to the accuracy or completeness of the contents of this book.

Cover Design: Catherine Clarke Design
Cover images courtesy of Sue Challis

In memory of Joyce and Harry Challis

Joyce's Family

Joyce, born in 1920, was the youngest of the four children of Nellie (b. 1881) and Alf (b.1879), who lived in Battersea in South East London. Her elder brother John was born in 1907 and sisters Did 1912 and Glad 1910. Alf was a porter at Clapham Junction Station on a very low wage which later was supplemented, as in many families, by a lodger, Cousin George, a soldier who survived the 1914-18 war and was able occasionally to obtain paid work as a dock hand. The family took a meal every day to bed-ridden Aunt Alice, who lived in the next road. Life was very much built around neighbours and family, hand to mouth with frequent use of the pawnbroker to level things up.

The family were exposed to the health-threatening impact of rats, human lice and fleas which were rife in the households, and to tuberculosis from which many of their neighbours died. Joyce herself spent three months in an isolation hospital ward with scarlet fever, which had a 25% mortality rate. Chapter 3 'Touch Yer Collar' is about that experience. As an adult she discovered she had childhood TB scars on her lungs. The title is a reference to a widely held superstition that prevented one being the next patient in a passing 'fever ambulance'.

The message that comes from Joyce's accounts is that family and community commitment, despite the appalling conditions, enabled a lively and happy childhood.

Introduction

Housing and social conditions in the London Borough of Battersea in the 1920s and 1930s were dire. Joyce Challis was born into this environment, in the ground floor of a tenement, with a second family occupying the top floor, a third family of ten living in the basement; all occupants sharing one tap and outside toilet. Within a few years, every one of the basement family had died of tuberculosis of the bowel.

Despite such hard living conditions, this community – especially its playground, the street – was a source of rich experience, fascination and fun for children like Joyce.

These stories written by Joyce in the 1980s are her account of her street experiences as a child and young adult. They have been compiled by her son and daughter since her death in 2004 with a minimum of editing, the only additions being the illustrations by her daughter. They describe the family loyalty and community commitment which were essential for survival during those unimaginably tough times, and which undoubtedly shaped the social and political commitment Joyce displayed in spades throughout her life.

Mike and Sue Challis

1

Sammonsie's Donkey

Directly across the street from us lived the Sammonsies. I suppose the name was really 'Salmon', but to us children and most of the grown-ups, 'Sammonsies' meant the house, the family, and everything concerning them.

Like all the houses in the street, it was shared between two families. The Sammonsies lived in the upper half. Although I had never been inside, I knew this because, in the long summer evenings, Mrs S, large and immobile, would sit at an open upstairs window, 'watching points', as my father would say.

The remaining members of the family were Mr S and Ginger-Cobb. Ginger's position in the family was never, as far as we children were concerned, clearly defined but we had the vague impression that it was that of son and heir. Whatever the case, he was always referred to by all and sundry as Ginger-Cobb – spoken as one word, like gingernut or gingerbread.

He was in his early teens and therefore already regarded as an adult. What is more, he had the unmistakable bearing of a man who, with no dependants, was in regular employment. He enjoyed the respect, curiously untinged by envy, of the less fortunate. In fact, when every Saturday night Ginger-Cobb emerged from No 32, spruce in navy blue, white shirt, collar turned neatly out and Oxford Bags flapping along with each bowed but purposeful step, he brought a sense of pride and security into our somewhat haphazard lives.

Sammonsie was employed too, but as he was a street trader, hawking fruit from his own donkey and cart, and as almost everyone else in the street was engaged in a similarly self-employed occupation (if they did anything at all), he received a lesser share of neighbourly reverence – a commodity that was never abundant anyway – than his junior.

And he hated kids. Not violently or even irritably, but with the dull loathing that a clean housewife might have for the soot from the railway running at our back.

This, of course, we knew. It had little effect on us. In fact, it made life – interesting enough in itself – even more interesting, because the reason for his hatred, and reason enough as I see it now, was that Sammonsies had a donkey.

We were familiar with many horses, although not of course with the easy confidence of country children. There were still a good many used on the roads, in those days. We stole many illicit lifts hanging on to the backs of the baker's light van, the coalman's cart, and the brewer's dray. We earned the curses of the iceman who delivered large blocks of ice to the fishmonger and the butcher, by scrambling right up onto his cart, after chips of ice, and sitting just under his wheels to spit out the grit when all the 'flavour' had been sucked out.

Especially interesting and exciting was that the donkey lived in our street. Sammonsies was a replica of every other house in the street, with the exception that there was a narrow alleyway between it and the house next door. Only the Sammonsies and Old Coalie had an alley and the reason for the alleyways' existence remains a mystery. Every house for miles around was part of a terrace and, even if you happened to be the lucky inhabitant of an end house in such a terrace, ten to one the outside wall would be stuck onto that of a Mission Hall or the gasworks. Alleyways were in short supply in our neighbourhood and we could only surmise that an unusually benign landlord had left these gaps between the houses in order to give to our part of the street a little more opportunity for variation and entertainment. At least, that was the result of it, because across this gap and at a slight angle, Sammonsie had nailed a piece of corrugated iron. At back and front he had contrived, with the aid of a steady supply of orange boxes, walls and a door – a stable: rough, but adequate – or almost adequate, because the door possessed neither lock nor key, but only a rusty iron bolt on the outside. We were not bad children. Adult authority was firm and, what is more, united. We were a source of annoyance, not only to our own families but to everyone who lived nearby, so a cuff round the ear was not considered the sole prerogative of the recipient's parents, whose general comment was that we must have 'asked for it'. Nor were we bored or looking for trouble. Traffic had not yet eliminated our street playground and adventure and excitement there was in plenty.

Therefore when we were gathered, as we often were, before the door of Sammonsie's donkey stable, the idea of interfering in any way with his master's arrangements for his comfort and security seldom occurred to us.

Perhaps there is something deep within a donkey's inner self which gives it faint intimations of the coming spring. Whatever the reason, sometimes in the spring, Sammonsie's donkey would 'kick up' and if we were there, we would shout a little encouragement, and he would respond delightfully.

My father said that one day he would "kick the bloody door down". We fervently hoped that this would one day come to pass.

So one evening, when we realised that the door was always going to hold, we started to egg on the boldest of our gang, Syddy Rolls.

And on that fine spring Saturday evening, Syd slipped the bolt. If ever there was a collective effort, it was that final act. For a moment we froze, horrified at the extent of our own daring. Then we scattered, and within seconds were squatting innocently on our own doorsteps, lying along copings, or swinging on iron gates – casual, but watchful.

There was a long, tense silence, broken at last by a great thud – and Sammonsie's donkey emerged, behind-first! He sniffed the air a bit, turned round once or twice as if to find his bearings, and then made the glorious bolt. Up the road he went, tail flying, with a score of us after him.

"Sammonsie's donkey's out!"

What joy! What exquisite happiness! At the corner he stopped suddenly and turned to face us, head down, and Sammonsie came down the steps of No 32, like the leader of a lynch mob, with murder in his eyes and a rope in his hand. At his master's approach, down onto the ground went the donkey, kicking his legs and braying like mad, and down on the ground went we kids, shouting with helpless laughter and kicking our legs too, in sympathetic ecstasy. He brayed, we brayed, and echoing down the street went the shout, "Sammonsie's donkey's out!"

Windows flew open; the population emerged from front doors and scrambled up area steps; relatives and friends were fetched from nearby.

Old Mrs Collins, who was paralysed and lived in the basement of No 16, was carried up, chair and all, and there she sat in the sunlight, blinking her eyes and smiling amiably at the women. The show then flew past: donkey, kids, and poor old Sammonsie. Seeing for the first time the reason for her resurrection, Mrs C added her old high voice to the tumult, "Oh, my Gawd! Those kids! It'll be the death of me!"

At that moment, the donkey, hemmed in now on both sides, mounted the pavement and plunged blindly into the public bar of the Shakespeare. He backed out immediately, followed by half a dozen patrons and our yells of, "Give him a pint, he wants a pint!"

But they didn't give him a pint. Instead, as they always did on such occasions, the adults began to get organised. The able-bodied men in their shirtsleeves and braces began to surround the animal: coaxing, pleading, and cunningly advancing.

We were all on the donkey's side, hoping he would never be caught. We willed him with all our might to greater excesses. We wanted him to knock them all over, to charge up the high street, creating lovely chaos, to devour all the fruit from the barrows, to jump over the moon!

He never did these things, but he did have one or two men on their backs. He knocked all the placards down from outside the sweet shop; he kicked Foxy – the bookie's runner – a lovely one in the solar plexus, and all this was sweet to us.

At one stage, a policeman on his beat came on to the scene. This, we thought, was more like it. Perhaps he would join in and suffer the same ignoble defeat as had our elders. But no... he was a shrewd officer, old on the beat, quickly recognising this as one of the many situations where the authority of the law is best upheld by a dignified and unhurried retreat. So his appearance, apart from the sudden exit from the scene of one or two of its participants, had little effect. And there was the donkey, head down, heels up, chasing Old Sammonsie into the rag and bone yard.

We wanted it to go on forever, this glorious happening which was beyond the control of all our adults, and indeed it may well have if it hadn't been for Ginger-Cobb. Because Ginger, as well as being the champion lightweight amateur for south west London, and having a regular job and courting steady, could handle the donkey.

So when he could be found – he'd been training up the park, they said – it meant the end.

He came into view, swaggering unhurriedly down the road, rolling like a sailor, all five-feet-two of him. He took the noose from the old man's hand, approached the animal, whistled softly between his teeth and slipped the rope over the submissive head. Just like that. It was all over.

Old Mrs Collins was carried down again and the women scurried inside their houses, leaving the men standing around in groups... while we cleared off quick, in case we were called in to bed.

2

Expedition with Lally

I don't know how old Lally Mills was; about seven or eight, perhaps. It was hard to tell really, because she had such an old face, although her body was that of a child. She spent her time in the well of one of those high prams with the huge wheels and, with her skinny arms and legs waving about all over the place, looked all the world like a big spider trying to get off its back. I heard the grown-ups say that she had rickets, but as the rest of the Mills family looked extremely robust and Jackie, their youngest, had a habit of eating what looked like a pretty substantial dinner on his knees on the front pavement for all to see, lack of food was not the most likely cause of Lally's problem. We certainly never heard of any medical diagnosis, or of her receiving treatment.

Lally was a sort of mascot for the children who lived by her. She was probably put into the care of one of her many brothers or sisters but the responsibility for Lally was taken on by all of us. We never went anywhere without her; in fact, there was often competition for the job of pram-pusher. We played lots of games that involved teams lined up on the pavement each side of the road and if you had obtained the job of pram-pusher and had to run to the other side, Lally came too. In spite of the bumps and the danger of being pitched out, she seemed to enjoy it. And when there were no children playing out, Lally's pram could always be seen outside the house, where the occasional passer-by – child or adult – would give her a prop up and coax a smile from her little monkey-like face. She was never short of treats either. When sweets, oranges, and even bread and black treacle were being shared, 'give Lally a bit' was the rule. Even Johnny Rolls – who always begged your discarded orange peel and would stare patiently at you as you ate your apple before muttering his "Giss yer core!" – would offer a share of his scavengings to Lally.

So, when Doughnut offered to show us the way to the 'real' country, Lally naturally came with us. Doughnut's Mum called him Dickie so, when he first arrived as a newcomer to our area, we initially christened him 'Dickie Doughnut' as a matter of course. This was later shortened to Doughnut and, to his more intimate friends, Dough or even Old Doughy.

We were sitting in a row along the kerb outside the corner shop, watching Doughnut and Syd Rolls playing a desultory game of cherry-bobs. It was the first day of the school holidays and our expectations were high. "We could all go to the real country, where I used to live," announced Doughnut.

Syd looked up from the game and Doughnut gave his cherry stone an extra surreptitious shove. "Wherezat?" Syd asked. "Richmond Park, not far. I know the way there."

We stood up, surrounding Doughnut.

"A park's not real country," we chorused.

"This one is. It's a park in the real country. It's called Bushy."

A wide expanse of green shrubbery and dense fern, a paradise of dens and secret hiding places, grew before our eyes. Our imaginations were fired by acres of tall trees, each with a set of firm and accessible boughs inviting us to climb to the very heavens. "Let's go!" we shouted.

There were seven of us when we set out, not counting Lally or Baby Billy Rolls, who had graduated into a wooden pushchair, a deckchair-like structure on wheels, in which he sat as fat and immobile as ever, complete with dummy and clutching a rag doll of a universally grey colour in his fist.

Rosie Mills had charge of Lally's pram at this stage, with young Jackie clinging, under the threat of dire punishment if he dared let go of the handle. Syd and Doughnut took the lead.

"You follow me, you lot," beckoned Doughnut. Syd, sensing a deeper challenge, gave Doughnut a nudge to the side of the pavement. "I know the way, too, Dough. I'm in front."

We proceeded up the road towards Wandsworth High Street, the power struggle up at the front somewhat impeding our progress and not helped by Syd's frequent pauses caused by his boots, which – several sizes too big and without laces – were frequently left behind, on the pavement.

"Everybody keep your eyes open for a bit of string," suggested Rosie, for the umpteenth time watching Syd hopping back and forth on his sockless feet.

Syd, however, with characteristic enterprise, popped into a tobacconist's and came out with a yard or so of white string; a commodity that was in plentiful supply in the days before Sellotape and cardboard packing cases.

We all waited while Syd sat on the kerb and threaded the string through the lace holes of his boots. He shuffled around a bit until he declared himself satisfied with their comfort and we carried on walking until we reached the crossroads at the end of the High Street.

"We have to go up a hill next," directed Doughnut.

"Can't see no hill," commented Rosie Mills. She played safe, however, offering, "Here, who wants a go at pushing Lally?"

Bella Baker let go of my arm, took the handle of the pram, and good-naturedly followed the rest of us up a side turning. After a few yards, we slowed down. There was a chorus of complaint from the group. "We're lost!"

We were about to enter unknown territory. Doughnut went back and grabbed the handle of Lally's pram. "No we're not."

Pushing Lally, he took the lead. He moved confidently along the pavement and we reluctantly followed. The turning was characteristic of most of those in the area. A corner shop, rows of unkempt terrace houses, a desolate-looking horse, head down, standing between the shafts of a cart and a little group of men playing pitch and toss on the pavement.

Also, a dozen or so strange kids.

They stopped playing as we walked towards them and stood silently watching us. Doughnut summed up the situation immediately, took a deep breath, shoved the pram towards the pitch and toss players and stood in between them and the wall, trusting to the protection of the grown-ups.

The eldest of the strange gang picked up a football from the road and advanced menacingly towards us.

"I wanna go home!" whined young Jackie.

Syd stood a while, assessing the relative chances we had in either running or standing to fight, what with our little band being composed mainly of girls and babies, although Bella, my best friend, and I could put up a tidy show when cornered. Syd took the diplomatic line.

"Clear off, round your own street!" Football took a step or two nearer.

Syd turned round to take the handle of the pushchair from Rosie. "Here," he said, meeting the enemy halfway across the road, "do you know where this kid lives? He's lost. We're looking for his mum." He indicated Baby Billy sitting placidly sucking his dummy. "We've been to the police station and they said he lives round here."

The gang, sufficiently interested in the incident of a lost baby, and deciding that our business was of a legitimate and even semi-official nature, watched us move away up the street.

"You told a fib, Syd," accused Bella.

It wasn't until we'd straggled through several similar streets that Doughnut seemed to become a bit subdued. He stopped boasting of his exploits in the dens and hideouts, rivers and trees of his former home and there was a hesitancy in his steps that soon revealed the cause of his gradual lapse into silence.

"You've been and lost us now, ain't you, Dough?" Rosie voiced our suspicions.

Jackie began to snivel again, "I wanna go home. I'm tired. My legs ache."

"Shut up!" Rosie commanded and picked him up, plonking him in the end of Lally's pram.

Syd walked on ahead and we shuffled along after him at a snail's pace. After a few minutes and a further couple of identical streets, Syd stood stock-still and beckoned us towards him. "We're there! Look!"

Through a narrow alleyway between the houses, we could see a wide expanse of green. Trees lined the path that ran through it and here and there were dotted little hillocks topped with scrub. We took the alleyway at a rush, yelling at the tops of our voices.

"Good old Dough!" Syd slapped him on the back as we tumbled in a heap onto the grass. "Come on, let's eat our grub."

We stayed in the same spot long enough to consume our jam sandwiches and empty our bottles of cold tea, then we moved off in great excitement to pastures new.

Bella expressed her delight with a perfect cartwheel.

"You've got a big hole in your drawers," said Rosie.

Racing up to the top of the nearest little hillock, we lay panting under the shade of a bush, looking up at the sky.

Presently, Doughnut stood up and reached into the top of the bush. "Here. What's this?"

He held a woman's small, black, straw hat in his hand. There was a blue ribbon round the brim and a spray of flowers on the front.

"It's a titfer," shouted Syd, snatching it out of Doughnut's hand and placing it on his own head. He danced up and down, pulling faces and singing in a high falsetto. "Where did you get that hat? Where did you get that hat?"

"Give us a go, Syd!" we clamoured. Jackie put it on back to front and copied Syd's song, while Bella and I simpered about in it, mimicking models and talking in posh voices. Rosie declined to take part, suggesting alternately that the lady would come back for it in a minute, and that it probably was full of fleas. How the hat got there is a mystery but what happened to it was decided by Lally.

She had been sitting up in her pram, wriggling with excitement and pleasure at our clowning, and now, straining her body upwards, she reached out a little brown claw for the hat. We all darted over to Doughnut, who was busy waving the hat about on the end of a stick, whipped it off, and sat it carefully on Lally's straight brown hair.

"There," said Rosie, forgetting her previous objections.

Syd took Baby Billy's dummy out and replaced it with a medicine bottle of cold tea. Straightening up, he demanded, "Come on then, where's the river, Dough?"

Doughnut pointed vaguely in an easterly direction and we gambolled off again to a clump of trees through which we could glimpse water.

There we discovered a small pond, covered in algae and deep with mud and before you could say Jack Robinson, we were in it, Bella, Rosie and I taking our shoes and socks off and the others wading in, boots and all. Lally sat watching us in her new hat, her pram standing side by side with Billy's pushchair, while we girls and Doughnut kicked up the muddy water and Syd stood up to his thighs in the middle of the pond.

He gave a sudden shout. "Here, you lot!" Syd came splashing his way out, his trousers covered in green slime, "Look over there. There's the horspidal."

He ran up and down, stopping every now and then to stare in front of him, shaking his head as though he couldn't believe his eyes. A tall, white building accompanied by the characteristic laundry chimney stood not more than a few hundred yards in front of us.

As though they had only just materialised, other familiar landmarks began to appear. The exciting little hillocks became those we'd played on a hundred times; the gas container on the horizon the one I could see from the window of my classroom; the pond the very one that we'd fished in for tadpoles ever since I could remember.

We looked at each other. "We're on the bloomin' common," we breathed, incredulous.

3

Touch Yer Collar

Touch yer collar,
Never holler,
Never get the fever!

We stood in the middle of the road and watched the ambulance disappear in the direction of the High Street. We had seen the ambulanceman enter the Bignalls' house and carry Sally Bignall, wrapped in a thick red blanket, down the steps and into the ambulance. Now the street was unusually quiet. A few women had stood in little groups on the pavement, talking softly, then had broken up to go back indoors. Rosie, Syd and the rest of us had stopped playing as soon as the ambulance had entered the street and were still standing motionless, hands on our collars.

"She's got the diphtheria," announced Rosie, who knew everything. She pushed us up onto the pavement as the baker's cart came briskly round the corner and we moved over to the wall next to Welman's, the corner shop. Mrs Budd's house was adjacent to the shop and we stood just beneath her window. She poked her head out of the front door. "Shove off, you lot, go down your own end."

We moved off a foot or two until we heard the sound of her door closing and then resumed our original stand. Syd sat down on the pavement, his back against the wall. He started to idly pull lengths of wool from the hole in the elbow of his jersey and wind them round his knee.

"I've 'ad that."

We sat down beside him and he looked along the row.

"What?"

"Diphtheria AND empitiger. I went in an amberlance like that."

Dolly, Syd's younger sister, stood up, hands on her hips. "You didn't!" she yelled, "You're telling lies. You've only had the empetiger when they put all that mauve stuff on your face an' when you had that bead stuck up your nose Mum took you to see Aunty Vivi in a pram. I know 'cos I came too wiv my sores. You ain't never been in an amberlance!"

She moved away, out of Syd's reach.

In the face of this testimony, Syd muttered something about "before you was born", and swiftly changed the subject. He rose and hitched up his shorts to knee level, like a sailor starting up the Hornpipe.

"Who's got any rope?"

Jackie Mills scrambled to his feet and dashed across the road to number 49. While we waited, Sammonsie the greengrocer led his donkey down the road, pulling his cartload of fruit and vegetables. They came to a halt outside his house and Sammonsie disappeared into his lean-to and brought out a nosebag, leaking oats all over the pavement. While the nosebag was being secured, the women began to trickle out of their houses, carrying shopping bags. Mrs Budd, dressed in the ubiquitous crossover apron, an old grey cardigan covering her shoulders, emerged from her street door a few yards to our right. She waved her shopping bag at us. "Shove off, you lot. Down your own end," she repeated.

Jackie stood in the middle of the road with a length of yellow hemp rope in his hand and we joined him there.

By the time we were ready to start our game of 'Fishes in the net', another four or five children had joined us. Syd held the rope and at his signal we all scattered. His task was to catch us one by one, tie each child into the net and drag his 'catch' around until all had been caught. The excitement was high and the noise ear-splitting. Syd had caught almost all of us when his mother, with her sacking apron round her huge girth and a man's cap on her head, came to their door to let out the clarion call she always used to gather her large flock.

First the words, "You young!" were uttered in a low mezzo soprano, then came the first syllable of the child's name, a little higher in tone, with the last syllable gradually rising to a crescendo and finishing on a top C. As Syd was usually the last to obey the summons, "You young... Syd-ee!" was repeated several times a day, with any children who were around at the time joining in.

The signal reminded us that it was likely to be dinner time for all of us and we peeled off to our respective homes. Most of us had easy access to our houses. The method of entry was simple enough: a hole drilled through the door near the latch with a string threaded through and tied to the locking mechanism. A sharp tug would open the door immediately. As for night security, that was ensured by the use of heavy bolts at the top and bottom. There were no keys in our street. As I pulled at the string, I began to think about little Sally Bignall. The Bignalls were a young couple who rented a room in Number 26. Sally, always one of the neatest and cleanest of children in the street, was their first and only child. I wondered what it was like in hospital and whether my mother knew Sally had been taken there.

My sister Mary was sitting at the table waiting for her dinner when I went into the kitchen. It was half term and she had been helping my mother all the morning. There was plenty to do because Aunt Gertie and Uncle Eddie were coming to stay overnight at the weekend and that meant a double spring-clean. Even the lino had to be taken up and the boards scrubbed.

"You were supposed to be doing the toy cupboard out," accused Mary as I took my place.

She looked hard at me when I didn't answer, because I usually had a sharp retort to that sort of remark.

Mum put a plate of Irish stew and dumplings before each of us and sat down beside Mary.

"Go and wash your hands," she ordered.

I went into the scullery. The sight of the dripping tap brought on a sudden raging thirst and I dashed back into the kitchen for a cup. I emptied it twice before I sat down to my dinner and played around with it for a while.

"What's the matter?"

"Don't feel well."

"Come here." My mother put down her knife and fork and held her hand to my forehead. "Don't you want your dinner?"

"No. I'm too thirsty."

"You got a sore throat?"

I nodded, feeling her anxiety, and she began to undo the strings of her overall.

"Stay here," she ordered Mary, "I'm going for the doctor."

For the rest of the day, I lay on a blanket which my mother spread on the rag rug before the kitchen range. Consciousness came and went, interspersed by vivid dreams which ended in a terror that sent me screaming into my mother's arms.

It was evening before the ambulance came. A brief period of consciousness revealed the night sky and the dusky street, a white interior and a banging of doors.

"Why are you crying?" The voice was impassive, unconcerned.

"I want my mum."

"Well, you won't get her by crying. Drink this."

The nurse held my head while I took the water from a feeding cup. When it was finished, she walked away without speaking. I turned my head to look round the ward. Both sides were closely lined with beds and there were several head-to-foot in the middle of the floor. Everything was either white or shining: the nurses' uniforms with their huge winged caps; the curtainless windows reaching to the ceiling; the smooth bedcovers stiff with starch and gleaming floors. It was terrifying: antiseptic. I felt its menace and closed my eyes.

After days and nights of vivid dreaming and raging thirst, I was at last able sit up and take food. There were parcels and letters and other children who, able to walk, came to my bed. I hardly noticed them, staring for hours through the window opposite to a little bridge in the snow with real people walking over it and one night, when the ward was dark, a porter carried me wrapped in a red blanket through the corridors to an isolation ward, a glass box with a sink in which for hour after hour the tap dripped and it seemed that no one came. It transpired that in the pristine, sterilised atmosphere of the diphtheria ward, a scarlet fever bug lurked and I had taken it in. Anyway, most of the time I spent in the place I was on the verge of tears, much to the annoyance of the staff who probably expected a little more exaltation on my part, having been rescued from the jaws of death. They never got it and I remained their weeping willow until, nearly three months later, someone who said she was my mother came to take me home.

4

Old Coalie

Coal was relatively cheap in the 1920s and 1930s, but nevertheless many housewives bought it in the smallest quantities, one bag at a time, to match the size of their weekly budget. Our source of supply was Old Coalie. I don't know if he was in fact old but as anyone over the age of twenty-five or so had earned that title anyway, and because he wore a long black beard in a mostly clean-shaven community, and was frighteningly irascible, we children labelled him as ancient. He appeared to have very little to do with the rest of the street and lived entirely alone. Furthermore, he gave no consideration to the universal problems involving cash flow: there was no question of 'tick'. It was cash-and-carry at Old Coalie's, with cash unremittingly first. For this reason alone, he would have been unpopular with the grown-ups. We children, always looking for ways of making life more interesting, managed to build him up into a monster. In fact, he really did look like the giant in my copy of *Jack and the Beanstalk*.

Shouting, "Old Coalie eats coal, from a dirty pudding bowl!" down his area steps was considered one of the more daring of our exploits.

It was because of all this that being sent on an errand for a bag of coal involved decidedly mixed feelings. Old Coalie kept his supplies in his area basement, next door to the pub. There were half a dozen small trolleys there too, to take your coal away, with smooth wooden handles and two deliciously noisy wheels; so on the one hand there was Old Coalie putting the fear of God up us and on the other, the lure of the trolley, with turns each for you and your mates on the way.

It was on one such excursion that my friend Bella and I got a real fright. I arrived home from school and met my mother at the front door, just as I was about to pull on the length of string threaded through a hole in the door and tied to the latch inside. She had a bucket of water in one hand, which meant she was about to clean the windows, and a clean apron over her afternoon clothes. My mother did almost all of her housework in the mornings, except for the tail end of the washing, and all the ironing and baking, but the window cleaning, which she hated, was always an afternoon job. At about two o'clock every day, she would wash and change into a clean dress and, because window cleaning was a 'public' type of job, it also merited her prettiest fresh crossover apron.

Those housewives who took pride in the spotlessness of the vermin-ridden houses they lived in needed not only to be clean but to be seen to be clean to earn the universally recognised seal of approval for decency and respectability. We always thought my mother overdid it a bit and my father swore it was she who scrubbed the pattern off the old worn lino, not us children always running in and out of the street.

"Where have you been? It's gone four. I want you to run an errand," she said and, not waiting for an answer, she put the bucket down on the doorstep and took a shilling out of her overall pocket. "Get me a bag of coke-coal from Coalie."

She reached into her pocket again and brought out a halfpenny. "You can buy some sweets for you and Mary on the way back."

Coalie's wasn't more than a few hundred yards from our house, but to go any farther than the corner shop without company was more than any of us could bear. So I spent some minutes rounding up my friend Bella who, with the promise of a go on the trolley and a couple of sweets thrown in, was a more than willing companion.

We fetched the coal home all right and started back with the trolley, stopping at the sweetshop to spend the halfpenny – which proved our undoing. I tipped Bella out of the trolley before we went in to choose the sweets and stood the trolley up against the front of the shop.

Spending a halfpenny in our sweetshop was a more prolonged affair than you'd think. Not only were there scores of items that cost the whole amount, there were hundreds that cost even less. What seems amazing is that the shopkeeper had the patience to stand behind his counter for anything up to a quarter of an hour to earn whatever profit he made from the sale of a ha'porth of sweets. In our shop there was an element of chance too of exciting gain to be made with each halfpenny purchase. Mr Lovejoy had a small cardboard box on his counter containing a number of plain postcards. Each postcard was marked with an amount of money ranging from one halfpenny to twopence. The customer chose a card at random and was served with the sweets in the amount stated. Most of the cards showed a halfpenny, of course. I never won two pennyworth, although we heard of someone who did and once I got a penny one and Dolly Rolls three-halfpence.

Deciding which card to select was also time-consuming of course, and by the time we had come up with the usual halfpenny and changed our minds from four liquorice sticks to ten sweetheart shapes, and over to four gobstoppers and back again, we had been in the shop some considerable time.

And it goes without saying that, when we came out, the trolley had vanished.

Mum had finished washing the downstairs windows when we got back and was sitting outside on the windowsill cleaning those on the upper floor. I went upstairs and stood staring at her through the glass. She was gazing towards me but seeing only the smears and stains as she pushed the leather over the panes.

The window was pushed open wide and she dropped down into the room, wiping her face with the back of her hand.

"Mum, someone pinched the trolley!" It came out with a rush and my lip trembled.

"Wait a minute." She turned and closed the window with a bang. "What did you say?"

"The trolley's gone!" This time it was a shriek. She grabbed my dress at the back and pushed me downstairs while I wailed out the story.

"You should have waited until you had taken it back before you went for sweets, shouldn't you? Now go and look for it. Some little devils have got it. You find it!"

I wandered disconsolately out into the street and knocked at Bella's door but Bella, gobstopper still in mouth, found this errand less attractive and 'was having her tea', she said. Half an hour went by and although I asked several of the children playing in the street, no one had seen or heard anything of the trolley. I kept clear away from Coalie's in case he came up his steps and demanded his property and, trailing along the street, saw my mother on the doorstep. She was beckoning me towards her and I ran, the tears falling.

She opened her arms.

"Come on in. I've got your bread and jam. Leave it for a bit and go out again later. I'll send Mary with you."

When Mary and I, regaled with our bread and jam, ventured out in search of the trolley, our street was deserted. It was one of those periods in the life of the street, usually teeming with activity, when in a few moments all is quiet and there is no one to be seen for an hour or so. Front doors, often left open all day, were firmly closed; perambulators had been taken indoors or stood empty on the pavement. The factory hooters had not yet sounded and people were not yet on their way home from work. There was an empty, abandoned look to the street and Mary and I wandered away from it towards the high street.

We hadn't gone far, however, before we reached Sunshine Way. This misnamed thoroughfare was considered in the table of respectability as 'rough'. Not the 'roughest', but rougher than ours. Added to that, the children who lived in it were in a different school catchment area so were not our playmates. In fact, we considered them as complete foreigners. Alien, inimical, and, to be truthful, frightening.

As we reached the corner, we heard the Sunshine Way mob shouting and laughing in the road. We also saw the trolley being trundled along the middle of the road with a gang of five or six running along beside it. A big girl with a mass of ginger hair and boy's boots was sitting in it with her legs up in the air. They were having an uproarious time and it was obvious to us that they weren't going to tire of it very soon.

We approached slowly. As soon as we were

spotted, the game finished and the biggest girl in the group came towards us.

"Clear off!" she said.

Mary stood her ground and I got behind her.

"It's not your trolley!" Mary took a step towards it as it lay in the road.

"Tis!"

"Tisn't. You pinched it from outside Lovejoys!"

"Didn't! It's me dad's!"

The big girl took a menacing step towards Mary, but Mary stood her ground.

"Give us a go then," Mary challenged.

"Give us a go, then," mimicked the girl, holding her dirty dress by the hem and dancing round us.

A chorus of indignant shouts came from the others. "Nah! We ain't had a turn yet. Clear off!"

"Go on, give my little sister a go. 'Ere y'ar, swop you for a go." Mary held out two gobstoppers.

The girl threw a defiant glance at her cronies behind her. "Alright, then. Only one go, mind."

I sat on the trolley and Mary slowly pushed me down the length of the street, glancing disdainfully at the little knot of boys and girls standing at the kerb. At the end of the street, she turned and walked equally slowly back, passed the big girl, and went on to the end. At the corner she stopped, as if to turn the trolley. She had no such intention, however, and with a whispered "Hold on tight!" she turned the corner and, pigtails flying, started to speed off towards home.

I hung on for dear life. Mary ignored the bumps

and ridges in the pavements that, when we rode the trolley for pleasure, she was so careful to avoid. Each bump almost knocked me off my seat and I began to wonder if being caught by the yelling mob behind us wasn't the lesser of two evils. The din made by the trolley, the clatter of boots on the pavement from behind us, and the shouting, made passers-by turn and jump quickly out of the way. It seemed that nothing could stop us now. My sister was a year or two older than all but the biggest girl and we were gaining ground. I could see the pub on our block only a few yards away when the trolley suddenly stopped, sending me sprawling on the ground.

"I've lost my shoe! I've lost my shoe!" shrieked Mary, rushing to the kerb to retrieve it.

It was all up with us then. Ginger-hair caught up in seconds, the rest of the gang close on her heels. The mob surged round us, their hobnailed boots coming dangerously near, the girl screaming at Mary, "Give us that trolley! It's my dad's. Go on or I'll hit yer!"

My sister leaned away, flinched, but clung on to the trolley handles. The others became more menacing, stamping round us in a sort of war dance. "Go on! Hit her, Edie. Give her one!"

The two girls stood immobile, staring at each other. Ginger-hair took a step closer. Then, it seemed in a second, suddenly vanished.

I looked back over my shoulder. There they were, haring back along the pavement as though the devil were after them. I gazed after them, laughing with relief. "Cowardy, cowardy custard!" I jeered in a sudden spurt of bravery. "Look, Mary, they're running away!"

Mary remained strangely silent. Looking up as I climbed to my knees, I saw behind my sister a giant of a figure with a great black beard and piercing black eyes. His coal-black hands seem to be reaching down to me as he bent near.

Old Coalie grabbed the trolley. "Get off! Go on. Hop it!"

We did.

5

Miss Godwin

When she came to our door one day, a neat little body of a woman in her late twenties, I happened to be kneeling on the top step with my back to the street, working my elbows up and down in a fair imitation of somebody knitting. This was a favourite occupation. It compensated for the fact that Mary, four years older, could actually do it and I couldn't, and saved me the trouble of learning how to.

"Mum, someone at the door!"

My mother took in the clean neatness, the rolled umbrella, the battered suitcase standing on the step. She put on her best 'stranger at the door' voice. "Yes?"

"I wondered," said Miss Godwin, "if you'd got a room to let?"

Mother took her in, of course, as she always did as long as there was room. Everyone had a lodger, anyway, to help pay the rent and at that time we were between lodgers as you might say. So it suited us in one way.

Miss Godwin had been with us about a week

and was sitting round the kitchen range drinking tea with Mum when Mother said something that made Mary and me 'prick up our ears' (they never had far to go, of course).

"You are like that, aren't you?"

A long pause.

"How did you know?"

"I knew the first time I saw you on the doorstep."

"You didn't say anything."

"No, and you'd better not, either. Leave it for a bit."

We never did find out what was supposed to 'be left for a bit', although we knew well enough who was to be left in ignorance. My mother steered around my father's attempts at authority like a practised river pilot heading for the open sea.

In fact, Mary and I remained ignorant of what had to be 'left for a bit', even when six months later Miss Godwin went into the Waterloo Lying In Hospital with a sore throat and, much to our delight, came back with little baby Jenny.

We all loved Jenny, especially my father. He would take her in his big, rough hands and sing his three favourite tunes, the only ones in his repertoire and those he had sung over and over again to us. He began with "I'm Henery the Eighth, I am, I am", led up to "I'm getting ready for me Mother in Law, I'm getting ready for the fray," and finished on the quieter, more sombre note of "My coffin shall be black. Two angels at my head and feet, one to watch and one to pray. And one to wash my sins away." The last, sung as a sort of dirge, was guaranteed to quieten the most fractious of infants. It certainly did the trick with our Jenny.

So there we were; we'd acquired a new, lovely auntie, a real live baby doll, and, except for a rare pang of jealousy at being usurped from my position as youngest in the family, and having to sleep three in a bed, it all seemed most satisfactory as far as I was concerned.

It was Miss Godwin's unusual sensitivity to all our needs that had prompted her to try to teach me to knit during the very first week of her stay. She couldn't do that; it would have needed a genius for that task. I had five thumbs on both hands. Instead, she knocked four nails into a wooden cotton reel and showed me how to weave a multicolour length of wool from it. I was able to do that on the doorstep, actually facing the audience.

And that same week, Miss Godwin got herself a job. A fateful step if ever there was one.

I was playing in the street when my mother called me in. "I want you to take Miss Godwin up to Belchers and bring me back two three ha'penny soft-roe bloaters for your father's tea."

To Miss Godwin she said, "I know he was after someone to help in the shop. You might be lucky."

I felt proud to guide someone round familiar territory, and to show her the shop from which the Italian family sold ice cream and lemon ice wrapped in little cones of newspaper; the posh sweet shop where you could buy a whole tin of toffees for sixpence; and the butcher's where we bought our pease pudding and saveloys. "If I get this job," she said, "we'll all have some on the first Friday after."

Afterwards, we sat by the fire, holding bread on the long toasting fork against the bars of the grate. "I've got to go to see him after the shop's closed." She took a slice of bread from the table and fixed it on the fork for me. "If he wants me, I start on Monday."

So from then on, except for her spell in the Lying In hospital, Miss Godwin left home at seven in the morning and returned at seven in the evening. After the baby was born, she took her in the pram, and by the time Jenny was six months old, they'd moved in with Tom Belcher.

6

Britannia Rules the Waves

Miss Biggs, our class teacher, hitched up her skirt and sat on her desk in front of the class. She was a young teacher, new to the job, and the only member of the staff who used a table to sit on, showing her knickers. She was fresh and happy and full of ideas, and we loved her from the day we marched into assembly to her rendering of *Bye, bye, Blackbird* on the school piano.

"Next week on May 24th," she declared, tossing her bobbed fair hair out of her eyes, "is Empire Day, and we are all jolly well going to make it the best Empire Day the school has ever had. We have all been practising our songs and dances, your parents have been invited and now it is up to us. There will be some very important people here and we will show them how proud we are of our school and our love of our wonderful country."

We all sat up. Talk about Empire Day preparations or preparations for anything other than class lessons, was more than welcome. We searched our minds for questions to ask that might prolong the discussion until playtime.

Maisie Smith put her hand up.

"Will we be dressing up, Miss?" She knew darn well we would.

"Can our mums bring babies?" Elsie White's mum had no babies.

We managed to stave off most of the geography lesson, until Dolly Rolls overdid it with, "Will the King and Queen come to see us dancing?" and Miss Biggs twigged us and chalked up ten sums on the blackboard. We wrestled with them as the late spring sun streamed through the tall windows, thankful for the warmth after a cold winter when, with feet covered in chilblains, we scratched and fretted our way through the school day.

After play, Miss Biggs read us a story about a girl called Jo, who was brave and independent and clever, like Miss Biggs herself, while we dreamed and listened in a haze of chalk dust and sunlight. When we lined up to leave the classroom for home, Miss Biggs reminded us, "Don't forget, girls. Bring in the labels from the fruit cans that come from Australia, we shall stick them on the chart in Geography next week and talk about those people out there who will be celebrating Empire Day with us."

Our school celebrated Empire Day in style with all the parents invited, the piano out in the open and bunting festooned all over the iron school gates. It was held in the boys' playground with the mums leaning from the open windows high up on the walls of the London County Council school building, waving and clapping the performance down below.

Unfortunately, the programme was somewhat limited by the fact that everyone regarded the Australian, Canadian and New Zealanders as not having much culture to speak of, and the rest of the Empire being inhabited by 'Blackfellers' with only a few whites around to keep them decent. Our teachers had to train us with songs and dances from Britain. Mind you, they did this with a thoroughness usually accorded to the National Ballet. Our performance was almost faultless, and the limited nature of our repertoire merely reinforced our belief that we were the only lot who mattered anyway. In fact, to us, the run-up to the great day was entered into as if we were to be awarded a share of what was going from the pink bits spread all over the world map. To be connected, however tenuously, to the bonanza at the receiving end was enough for us and our rendering of *Land of Hope and Glory* was as enthusiastic as any from the playing fields of Eton.

Of our family, only Mary and I were still at school in the mid-1920s and Mary, four years older, was a member of the Scottish Dancing troupe. Inclusion in the various girls' dancing groups depended on what you were able to turn up in. Mary was with the Scots because she had a kilt which Mum had managed to find on Rolls' tot[1] barrow and, with a white blouse and a little black forage type hat that Ginny made, she shone. After the Scots, the standard fell a little. Teachers made half a dozen tall Welsh hats for a few of the girls but the other two groups, making do with a plenitude of waist aprons from home, were only distinguished by the choreography. This didn't matter to the audience of course, who clapped, and cheered themselves hoarse.

The younger ones, and that included me, were instructed to come dressed in red, white and blue, and all but a few managed this. My sister Ginny had become the family dressmaker as soon as she acquired a brand new Singer sewing machine for two shillings a week and was determined to do our family proud. I arrived in the playground in a flourish of red, white and blue flounces made of crêpe paper. It was easily the best rig-out in the school and I made the most of it, prancing and pirouetting around until Miss Pruit poked her bony knuckles in my back and sent me back into line.

Mr Grimshaw, the head of the boys' school, stood on a platform in the centre of the playground with the school lined up on all four sides. We waited patiently while he made an opening speech which sounded like *Land of Hope and Glory* in prose and then the singing started. The flags fluttered from the windows, the sun shone, we were bursting

---

[1] 'tot' being a second-hand clothes barrow.

with patriotic fervour and, what is more, we knew all the words. Our rendering of "We are the Yeomen, the Yeomen of England" with Miss drumming on the piano with gusto enough to shatter the instrument must have been heard up at the high street. At the last line, the first row of boys straightened up and lifted their hands in a smart military salute not at all spoiled by the bare elbows displayed through the holes in half-a-dozen jerseys. Neither did the lack of orientation in the infant school, whose role was to illustrate the line 'And foes to the right of us and foes to the left of us'. Our loyalty was unquestionable, our faith complete.

It lasted throughout an inaudible speech from an Important Person with no hair and a fat tummy, a couple of Scottish and Irish Reels, *Men of Harlech*, *Land of our Fathers* and, last of all, *God Save the King* (more elbows) from the whole assembly. Slightly drunk, we returned to our classroom, where Miss Biggs treated us to a gruesome story about a hole in Calcutta until the bell went for going-home time.

As we issued from the playground into the street, the sun disappeared behind a cloud and a chill breeze sprang up. I shivered in my paper finery and Dolly wrapped her grubby Union Jack round her shoulders. We waited for Bella, who was in a different class from ours, and felt the first few drops of rain falling on our heads.

Within seconds, we were caught in a deluge. We

stood against the wall while the rain beat down almost horizontally, filling our eyes and mouths, saturating our shoes and socks, running down our legs in streaming rivulets of icy water.

Hail peppered our arms and legs like gunfire for a few minutes and then stopped as suddenly as it had started. In the thin drizzle that was left, we started for home, Dolly's Union Jack clinging to her bony figure, the edges dripping water into her shoes, Bella's Welsh hat pulped to her streaming wet hair, the brim hanging round her neck like a halter. As for my finery, red, white and blue had become a streaky purple papier mâché, dripping mauve into my new white socks.

After a few yards of wet misery, trailing along down Musjid Road, the drizzle stopped and the sun reappeared. Within moments, the air became warmer and in a short while our clothes stopped dripping and started to dry. Bella threw her ruined Welsh hat to the kerb and Dolly wrapped her Union Jack up and carried it under her arm. As I wore only a liberty bodice and a pair of cotton knickers under my crêpe paper dress, modesty forbade any such simple resort and I shuffled along, wrapped in what felt something like a cold rice pudding.

Musjid Road led into Delhi Terrace, and a little row of shops. Judd's the Bakers stood on the corner and, cheered by the sight of the cakes in the window and the warm smell of baking bread, I followed Dolly and Bella to stand just inside the open door until Mrs Judd, standing behind the counter in her starched white apron, shooed us away.

Next door was the haberdashery and, as the shop door was closed, we passed it by without giving the shop keeper our habitual bit of cheek, but Isaacs' the tailor's, standing at the end of the row, had a bell on the door which gave a loud ping whenever it was opened, and that we seldom resisted.

We pushed the door. *Ping.*

Old Mr Isaacs came out of the back and into his gloomy shop.

"Go avay you kits." He advanced toward us, a menacing scowl on his face.

"Go avay!" mimicked Dolly and at the same time she gave me a push that sent me almost into Isaacs' arms.

The man held out his hands, shielding himself from the impact, and then pushed me away. I rushed out, tripping over a bale of dusty navy-blue cloth and falling on my face. I picked myself up and realised that I no longer wore the damp frock but stood in my purple underwear. Making for the door, I could hear Dolly and Bella repeating 'Old Ikey, the miser', as they skipped away. Following them, I glanced back to see Mr Isaacs standing outside the shop smiling benignly, offering the remains of the flounces to me in both hands.

7

Saturday Morning Pictures

Saturday morning pictures cost threepence, two in a seat, and most children somehow managed to go each week. Getting thruppence was the first job. Running errands, taking messages or minding babies could each earn fourpence a time. The most popular enterprise, though, was the returning of glass jam jars and newsprint to the wharf that stood on the banks of the Thames nearby.

On the waterfront, the great barges would be loaded with old newspapers and magazines and often, from our local recreation ground, we would stand and watch them floating down the wide grey river, the top layers fluttering in the breeze, merging with the flow of river traffic. On the land side, we would file into a huge cavern of a place, stacked to the ceiling with bottles and jars, old newsprint and rags, and offer our few jam jars at a farthing a time.

Early one particular Saturday morning, half a dozen of us gathered round Syddy Rolls, outside the corner grocery shop. We were off to get our money for the pictures and, incidentally, to play our part in the recycling business, although we may not have put it like that.

We were in various states of pecuniary. Bella had spent her penny pocket money, although she had intended to save it towards the pictures. I had three ha'pence, which I had managed to beg from my eldest sister. Jackie Mills said that he'd pinched tuppence; a statement which we refused to believe, and the Rollsies so far had nothing. But we had assets, and carried with us some bundles of old newspapers and our jam jars.

As usual, Syd was accompanied by Baby Billy Rolls. Baby Billy was seated, or rather squashed, into Syd's box cart, a soap box on four old pram wheels. He sat, propped up by an old pillow and covered with a scrap of blanket, as fat as a buddha and rendered as silent by a big rubber dummy stuck into the middle of his face. Baby Billy may have not grown out of his dummy but he had certainly grown out of his box. He looked as though he had been stuffed in, and perhaps he had, so maybe he couldn't have got out if he'd tried.

As for Syd, there was something about the leader of our little gang that could only be called charismatic. How this singular quality fought its way through the layers of his general appearance is a mystery. Like all the other Rolls children, Syd had shed his baby fat by the time he was four and had emerged as gaunt and skinny as a rake, probably an early symptom of the tuberculosis that was to wipe out almost the whole of the Rolls family before the end of the decade.

Anyway, dimples had given way to grubby tramlines, soft flesh to hard bone, submissive silence to, in Syd's case, a gravelly imperiousness. His style of dress certainly lent an air of singularity though, and was a source of admiration and envy.

The opportunity to choose one's own outfit, to wear whatever took your fancy, was usually confined to the adults, but Syd did this all the time. The reason for this sartorial affluence was Mr Rolls' occupation as a 'totter', shoving his hand barrow all round the posh houses of Clapham and returning at night with sufficient clothing for the whole street. For a few pence, Rollsie would sell you anything from an old pair of Wellington boots to a gold lamé dinner dress and, of course, his own family got first pick. And Syd had a real eye for quality, which he exercised with little regard for size or suitability.

We weren't a bit surprised, therefore, to find him that morning dressed in a man's evening jacket with silk lapels reaching down to his bony knees, with a surfeit of cuff and no buttons and a large, checked golfing cap aslant over one ear.

Dragging Baby Billy's box on a length of hemp rope, Syd led our little tribe to the riverside wharf. Baby Billy wasn't at all disturbed by our jam jars rattling round his podgy toes, but each time the cart left the kerb with an almighty jolt, and mounted the pavement on the other side of the road, out would come the dummy, and Baby Billy would let out a roar enough to wake the dead, whereupon we'd all come to full stop, Syd would retrieve the dummy, dip it into a tin of condensed milk, and shove it back into Billy's face. In the silence that followed, we'd all beg for a dip, only to be met with a firm refusal from Syd who, as though to reaffirm proprietary rights, would thrust his own forefinger into the tin, lick off the milk, wipe his fingers on his trousers, and off we'd go again.

Half past nine found us gathered outside the Hippodrome, pushing and shoving along with the other hundreds of patrons. There was no attempt to form us into a queue so for half an hour a mass of yelling, excited customers would mill around on the pavement until we were let in through the doors like Henry the Fifth's ragged army storming the breach at Harfleur.

It was a year or two before the great picture palaces, the Trocaderos and the Empires, but our local flea pit – as it was called – must have housed several hundreds.

On Saturday mornings, the little Hippodrome was staffed by the manager, who also served as the projectionist, and a man called Peggy who acted as the attendant or 'chucker out'. It goes without saying that Peggy, or 'Pegleg', was minus one leg which, to our delighted interest, had been replaced by one exactly like Long John Silver's. Peggy had no official uniform, no gold epaulettes or braided cap. On the other hand, being in charge of a mob of kids, offspring of an industrial working class well drilled in obedience and respect, such authority symbols were superfluous. In comparison with children of a later generation, our behaviour was impeccable and Peg's authority was unquestioned.

Once seated, the struggling mass of arms and legs, the screaming and the shouting, resembled nothing less than an indoor swimming pool, with Pegleg hauling the occasional miscreant out of the row, administering a violent shake, and tossing him or her back into the melee.

As soon as the lights went out and the initial deafening shout of "Hooray!" was over, however, things quietened down considerably. Audience participation was complete. Clapping and booing, stamping and shouting, cries of "Look behind you!" accompanied the exploits of Tom Mix, our favourite cowboy, Charlie Chaplin, Mickey Mouse and the terrifying Dr Fu Manchu.

We became more introspective when the love scenes appeared, of course, and attempts were made to continue the drama physically between the seats until something more interesting came up.

At a sign of real trouble, a serious fight, which was extremely rare, or the throwing of unacceptable missiles – orange peel and peanut shells didn't count – the screen would go blank, and the lights would go up, while the guilty party was swiftly and efficiently escorted to the exit.

So a good time was had by all (with the possible exception of Pegleg) except, were it not for our Syd's enterprise and initiative, on one occasion when things would have gone badly for our little gang.

On this occasion, a cry of "Peg, there's a lot of water on the floor!" brought him up to our row in double hopping time. He shone his torch onto the floor under our seats and signalled to the projection box. The lights went up – sure enough to reveal a stream of liquid running between Dolly Rolls' feet.

Dolly was hauled out into the aisle.

"You dirty little devil!" shouted Peggy, holding her by the neck of her jumper. "You've wet yourself, haven't you?" There was silence all around. This was even better than Tom Mix.

Peg started to push the now weeping Dolly towards the exit and naturally enough we stuck with her, following her woefully up the aisle.

Suddenly, Syd grabbed the back of Pegleg's jacket: "She didn't do it, honest!" He raised his gravelly voice. "It was a dare, I heard 'em." His accusing finger swept the row behind ours and rested arbitrarily on a little lad behind Dolly's vacant seat, at the same time grabbing his sister and shoving us all back into the row.

"It all ran down. Her drawers are dry, ain't they Doll? Come and feel, Peg!"

At that, Peggy, disconcerted by the invitation and by Syd's determined adherence to his reclaimed seat, lost no time in dragging the accused to the exit. The cinema echoed with loud protestations of his innocence as the lights went out and the unspeakable Fu Manchu tightened his stranglehold round the neck of his lovely victim.

8

Music Hath Charms

"I don't believe it! I just don't believe it!" Mum stood on the doorstep, seeing us off to school.

We followed the direction of her eyes and saw that what she just didn't believe was the sight of a furniture van standing outside the Mills's and two burly men struggling to carry a new piano up the broken front doorsteps.

Mrs Mills stood on the top step, a man's cloth cap flat on her head and little Beaty, her youngest, sheltered under the commodious shelf of her mother's bosom and clinging in panic to her grubby crossover apron.

"She had good reason to be frightened," said my mother at tea that evening, "they can't pay the rent now. Soon they won't be able to feed the kids."

"They look well fed enough at the moment," replied Dad, "Anyway, not paying the rent's different from not feeding the kids. Don't worry, as soon as they don't keep up the payments on it, they'll take it back."

He picked up the *Evening Standard* from the

chair. "See here, pianos from Ardinanobbs[2] or Hastings, two bob a week and when they don't pay, back it goes. They do it up and it starts all over again with another mug."

Mum stood up and refilled the big brown teapot. She poured my father a cup of tea and drew herself up tight. "Well, I wouldn't buy one."

"No, you're not daft. Besides, you can't play, can you?"

"Neither can any of the Millses," brother John put in, "nor the Elmers, or the Beals, and they've all got one. The only ones who can play theirs are the Caseys. They have a ding-dong every Saturday night."

"Don't we know it. Let's hope there's no one likely to turn out musical at the Millses."

John played an imaginary keyboard on the tablecloth. "You can pick it up, you know," he said, wistfully.

My mother looked across the table at her favourite. "I know, son," she stood up and began clearing away, "and you can pick up these plates, too, and take them out to the scullery. Come on, girls, you help him."

Our piano-possessing neighbours weren't the only ones whose musical ability was lacking.

---

[2] Arding and Hobbs, magnificent department store on corner of Lavender Hill and St John's Street, Battersea since 1876, a standard of unobtainable quality in 1925 and now 'reimagined to provide an engaging mix of retail and leisure uses'.

Perhaps the industrial revolution had helped to erase the fiddle and the pipes from our folk culture. Whatever the reason, except for a few cinema and pub pianists, there seemed to be few individual musicians among us. One or two of the men and boys had mouth organs and would sit at the corner of the street on sunny days and give us a version of *Danny Boy* or *Swanee River*. There were those, too, who could raise some sort of a tune from the Jew's Harp, and at parties there was always someone's uncle who would perform on the spoons, but that was all.

The streets, though, still provided us with some musical entertainment. As well as the barrel organ, which came round frequently and passed almost unnoticed by us, there were the performing ex-soldiers, men left over from the First World War and unemployed. Theirs was a show which no one would willingly miss, especially the children. We would rush around the houses with the news when we saw them coming round the corner, always in a great hurry, wheeling their piano on a cart.

The grown-ups would stand at their doorways or lean out of the windows and we children would sit in a prim line on the edge of the kerb, ignoring old Mrs Collins's regular cold weather chiding: "Stand up. You'll all get the pip in your bums!"

I suppose we'd call the performers drag artists now. In fact, my mother told us, they were the remnants of the concert parties the soldiers entertained each other with at the front. They took the parts of women, and sang in falsetto. It was a sort of burlesque, uproariously funny to us and probably risqué, although that would have gone clean over the heads of most of the kids. Anyway, we loved it. The dancing and singing, the intriguing sight of the soprano, leaning a muscular arm on the piano in between acts and smoking a Woodbine, with his old army boots showing beneath his tatty ballgown, drew ecstatic applause from us and, when the hat went round, an unstinting and completely sympathetic response from the grown-ups. In 1925, they were still 'our boys'.

There were street bands, of course. The most frequently heard was that of the Salvation Army, and my father, who was as musically illiterate as it is possible to be, would repeat the old cliché, "Whatever you think about them, they're fine musicians." They probably were, too.

The Boys' Brigade tried hard to provide some of the musical education completely lacking in the state schools. For a year or two, young boys would learn to play the trumpet and each Sunday morning would tour the streets on Church Parade, blowing loudly enough to wake the dead. Unfortunately, they seemed to blow themselves out of the organisation after a year or two when, I suppose, the girls became a new audience for another kind of trumpet-blowing that didn't go with the uniform. Sadly, they were obliged to give up their instruments to an organisation never flush in funds and for most, I imagine, that was the end of it.

It was the gramophone that really brought music to us. The old Music Halls were finished, sound pictures were in their infancy, but almost everyone had a gramophone. At first, we had only two records, great heavy 78s which revolved under a needle as thick as a bodkin. One was an instrumental rendering of *In a Monastery Garden* and the other an extremely vocal one: *I'm Barnacle Bill, The Sailor*. We had this latter record for years, even after we had acquired all Al Jolson's songs, Paul Robeson's, and later Gracie Fields'. And it was the gramophone which encouraged the one musical art which had never been lost. Everyone sang or whistled. The housewives sang their way round the house all day, and the men whistled or sang their way home from work.

There was little of the fine renderings you might find in the Welsh Valleys but there were some good untrained voices, and the new songs turned out by the embryonic Tin Pan Alley pop industry supplied us with plenty of new material, much of it of the *Keep your Sunnyside Up!* variety, to prevent us feeling too sorry for ourselves.

It was a matter of honour among us children to learn the words of the latest song immediately it came out, and I was no exception. But Barnacle Bill, played a thousand times over, remained my favourite and so, when one Friday afternoon, the day before the summer holidays, we were all assembled in the school hall for an impromptu concert and allowed to choose our song (an unusually liberal concession), he was my choice.

The girl who was chosen to sing before me had just returned to her place after what I secretly thought was a soppy song and I stood on the platform, word perfect and arms akimbo:

"I'm Barnacle Bill from over the sea
I'm Barnacle Bill the Sailor
I'm all dressed up like a Christmas tree
I'm Barnacle Bill the sailor."

So far, it was going down well, and Miss Pruit nodded her head in smiling condescension.

"*I'll come down and let you in*
Cried the fair young maiden.
(Bill stuck out his chin and continued)
Well, hurry before I break the door,
Cried Barnacle Bill the Sailor.
I'll break the door, I'll climb the stairs
And if I catch you unawares
You know a sailor never cares!...
Said Barnacle Bill, the Sailor."

There was a short silence and Miss Pruit came up onto the dais and stood in front of me, facing the audience. "Well, we shall end the concert now. Thank you those gals who sang the nice songs."

It was years before I suspected that I hadn't been included in that category.

9

The Taj Mahal

I think it was about 1926 when Cousin George came to live with us. He'd been a private in the Indian Army for years, although as far as I can remember, he was quite young, under forty, anyway.

While he was with us he'd have frequent bouts of malaria: a legacy from his army service. This meant that a high fever and dreadful shaking and trembling would lay him up for as long as two weeks. When this happened and he stayed upstairs in his room, I had the job of taking him bowls of bread and milk, the panacea for all convalescence in our house – besides Bovril, for really severe cases. I never liked the job.

"Why can't Mary go?" I'd ask.

"Mary's running the errands, you know that. Go on, up you go –" Mum would thrust the white pudding basin into my hands – "and don't spill it."

"I don't like that smelly old room."

"Don't be rude... up you go!"

All the windows at the back of our house were kept tightly closed. The shunting yards of the

London Midland and Scottish Railway ran a few yards from our back fence and the air was black with soot. And so were we, and everything that we possessed if as much as a crack appeared in the defences. So, what with the lack of fresh air, the foetidness of the malaria and Cousin George's cigarette smoke, my reluctance to administer to the sick was understandable.

"You can play with the Palace when you get up there," my mother would cajole.

Looking back, 'the Palace' must have been a model of the Taj Mahal, one of the many pieces of loot the British army brought back from India. I didn't know that then, but fully appreciated the exquisite ivory carving, its delicate filigree and perfect contours. It was so beautiful, and so different from anything I'd seen before, that I longed to touch it and to feel with my hands the little white elephants which stood in file along the narrow mantelpiece over the little grate, and to peer into the ivory lace of the carved Howdahs on their backs.

As I never ventured beyond the bed which stood just behind the door, I didn't get the chance to do just that, but always promised myself that one day, when circumstances allowed, I would.

When Cousin George became our lodger, he'd just left the army and was full of tales of the exploits and adventures he'd taken part in. I thought they were pretty dull on the whole, consisting mainly of hard and pointless tasks, suffering the punitive discipline imposed by the NCOs and countless hours of playing card games in unbearable heat. He was tall and upright though, with a cheerful self-regard which made him popular with the neighbours and in the pub.

It seems, however, that the army hadn't done much to equip him for civilian life, because as well as leaving him frequently out of condition with the malaria, he'd emerged without skills or experience which could help him earn a living.

So after a few weeks with us, when he lived like a king on some sort of bounty, George became one of the one-and-a-half million men who were more or less permanently unemployed and one of the thousands of unskilled men who sought work in the London dockyards.

This wasn't easy, partly because almost any man was as good as the next when it came to lugging goods to and from the ships to the quays, and only the stevedores needed the skills that stowed the cargo safely. Cousin George however, like the disciplined soldier he was, had at least learnt patience and every single day for two years, between sitting up in bed convalescing on Mum's bread and milk, he would be up at six-thirty to report for the Call In at the Surrey Docks.

The Call In was the method used to employ casual labour at the wharves. The men were employed for only the day they were taken on, and at seven-thirty each morning, George would join a crowd of others at the dock gate. The men, desperate for even one day's work, would shout and jostle to catch the foreman's eye. Those who were called slipped under the chain which was stretched across the entrance, leaving the rest to try their luck at the next Call In.

And almost every day, Cousin George would be back indoors by eight-thirty.

Then, one morning, he was still in bed when we came downstairs.

My father sat down to his fried egg. He took a forkful to his mouth and looked at my mother. "What's up with him, then ... another bout?" There was a note of accusation in his voice.

"I dunno." Mum feigned indifference.

Dad took the bread finger Mary was holding out and absentmindedly dipped it into his egg. "Nip up and see," he ordered me.

Reluctantly, I did as I was told.

"Are you awake, Cousin George?"

A muffled voice came from under the bedclothes.

"Have you got the 'laria?"

"No, off you go."

I held my breath and took my customary long look at the Taj Mahal and the little elephants, then reported downstairs.

When Dad went up, Mary and I put our hands over our ears as the shouting started.

I heard the words, "Ten bob a week, that leaves you with seven for yourself out of your dole money. This week you can make it fifteen." And then the terrible ultimatum, "Or get out!"

We started to cry and Mum took us into the scullery and closed the door.

All that day and for many days afterwards, Cousin George stayed in bed, surreptitiously fed by Mum. This meant plenty of trips upstairs for me while Mary, whose job it was to run the errands, brought back five Woodbines each day.

I suppose you can get used to anything in time, and after a few days, I didn't even notice the smell in George's small room.

"Here are your fags, Cousin George," I'd say.

George would take the tin foil that Mary always brought back from the tobacconists. Customers who smoked the more expensive brands saved it for George and he'd wrap it round the huge ball of foil he'd had for years. It was as big as his fist, and as heavy as lead.

"What will you do with it?" I once asked, fingering the tiniest elephant. I took the little ivory piece over to the window. "It's like a cannon ball. You could drop it out of the window and hit a train, couldn't you?"

I watched the great engine shunting trucks back and forth along the line.

"I could drop it out of the front and hit old Mother Bilson," said George.

We laughed.

"She hates us kids."

"She hates everybody."

After a while I ventured, "Cousin George! Why don't you get up and come downstairs?"

"Mind your own business. You go down if you

want." He took a dog-end from behind his ear, "Chuck over those matches."

"I mean you won't get taken on if you don't go to the Call In."

He didn't answer, but the next day he came into the kitchen just after Dad had left for work. And when my father came home in the evening, he brought some hopeful news.

Dad said nothing as he passed us on the way to the scullery to wash his hands. Mary and I searched his face for some sign of approval at George's resurrection. None came, and it wasn't until he had finished his tea and lit his pipe that he announced, "Old Jack says he'll take you round in the van. See if there's anything doing out a bit, over the water."

Old Jack wasn't all that old, but earned his title as an endearment for being my father's best buddy. Dad had been loading and unloading Jack's van ever since he first became a goods porter. Jack drove the distribution van for the railway company, touring all the London docks, warehouses and factories.

"Keep it to yourself. If the Company finds out, Jack'll be in trouble."

"What time?"

"Be at the Depot at eight o'clock. Tomorrow's Saturday, the gaffer won't be in." He picked up his copy of the *Evening Star* and began to study the list of winners on the back page.

"Looks as though we've had a bit of luck, gal," he said to Mum, his eyes still on the paper.

"Brighteyes came home at four to one."

"How much did you put on?" ventured Cousin George.

"A tanner. Half a crown for a tanner, that's two bob and me tanner back. Not bad."

George relaxed a little in his chair. "Thought it was a right outsider."

"Yeah, but he did well at Newmarket last week. What do you think about Blue Peacock in the three-thirty tomorrow?"

Basking in the easiness of this discourse, Mary and I went to sit on the rug at Dad's feet.

"I'll tell you what," he said, ruffling my hair, "Jack says you can come too as you're such a little'un. Nobody will see you sitting up the front."

Before we left in the morning, Mum gave George a clean white muffler and, as we left the house, he put on his best cap. There was a uniformity about men's clothes then: a thin cloth jacket, a waistcoat, a collarless shirt – usually of rough flannel and fastened with a collar stud – finished off with a white rayon muffler.

George, however, with his straight back and soldierly stride, stood out from the rest. It was difficult to recognise in him the dismal creature of the last few weeks and marching with him under the railway arch at the Junction, I felt proud to be holding his hand.

The depot was familiar territory. My father had worked there as a goods porter ever since he graduated from his first job as a van boy. He earned a few extra shillings on Sundays, feeding and watering the carthorses the Company used to haul the heavy coal carts, and he often took us along with him. We would be lifted up onto the gentle beasts and we'd be led for a little way round the yard past the bunkers of coal, sniffing up the mingled smell of coal dust and horse dung.

Jack was right when he said that I was unlikely to be seen up in the front of the van. Besides, it was Saturday; a working day until one o'clock for most, but a day when upper supervisory staff were thinner on the ground. So I sat on a pile of coal sacks between Cousin George and Jack and could just see over the dashboard. And once Tommy, Jack's van boy, had jumped onto the tailboard and was clinging to the rope that hung from the ceiling of the van, we were off.

"I've only got one delivery. Once we get over the water, we'll make for the Indian. I've got a couple of mates there, might be something doing for you," said Jack as we swung out of the yard and headed for the river. "First we'll take in the Wapping lot. I'll take her through the Borough and over London Bridge. We'll get rid of the load at Wapping, then we'll try the Indian, and we might even get to Tilbury if there's time. Be a bit of a way out for you there, but it might be worth it."

I strained to see the river as we drove over the bridge. It is strange to think that, living so near its banks, we seldom caught a glimpse of it except from our local rec, where a small space between the warehouses and factories had been reserved for our playground. So I was as excited as any country child to see the river frontage with the great ships and barges, the tall cranes and the wharves bustling with activity, loading and unloading to and fro from ship to warehouse, the dockers carrying the most incredible weights on their heads and shoulders.

George pointed out the children playing in the grey mud. "Tide's out. Your dad used to be a mudlark, you know. He was born in Wapping. Used to dive off the steps at Wapping Old Stairs after pennies the toffs threw in, didn't he, Jack?"

"So he says," replied Jack.

The 'Wapping lot' turned out to be the London Dock. Jack drove the van into the yard to the transit sheds and lifted me down. He pointed to the wide stone base on the warehouse wall and showed me the fossilised ammonite embedded in it. "The people who built this place left the fossils in the stone and cut round them to show them up more. Must have had plenty of time, then, eh, George?"

We made a royal entry through the noble gates of the West India Dock and, as we waited for a dray pulled by two shires to make its exit, George read out the words inscribed on the stone pediment above us: "The West India Import Dock. Began 12th July 1800. Opened for business 1st September 1802."

"They got a move on in those days," remarked Jack.

He put me down while they disappeared into the warehouse and when they emerged, Jack had a string of milky white crystals in his hand. "What d'you think this is, little'un?" he asked.

I shook my head.

"It's unrefined sugar, or halfway there. They refine it in the Commercial Road. Here, that'll keep you quiet for a bit." He heaved himself up into the driver's seat. "Can you smell the ginger and the nutmeg?"

We stopped at several docks before we reached Tilbury, where we watched the dockers carrying great long planks of wood by the half-dozen on their shoulders.

"I reckon meat's the worst," remarked George. "Nothing worse than a carcass of chilled New Zealand lamb. I've been at that for nine hours. You know it after that, I can tell you."

By one o'clock, we'd been from the London to Tilbury with me doing my best to break every tooth in my head on the rock-hard crystals. George had had no immediate luck but as Jack said, 'a word had been dropped here and there'.

Now it was dinnertime and, on the way home, we drew up at Mick's Coffee Shop in Rotherhithe. We sat between the high wooden backs of the benches and ate our steaming sausage and mash from the scrubbed tables while Tommy teased me. "If you put those sausages single-file on your plate and eat up the first one, the others will all move up. They make them here out of old cab horses. True, my dad told me." He reached over the table, holding his fork over my plate.

"Leave her alone," ordered Jack. "Get on and eat your grub."

The factory sirens for knocking-off time were sounding as we drove through Lambeth among the crowds of men and women on bicycles and on foot streaming from the factory gates.

As we pulled the string that opened our front door, Mary came up the steps behind us.

"D'you want this?" I offered her the remains of my rock crystals. "It's a bit sticky."

"Yuk!" responded Mary.

George resumed his seven-thirty Call In at the dock gates from then on. Each night Dad came home without much to offer from Jack's enquiries and after a while George stopped asking. Then, one Friday, he came downstairs with a parcel wrapped up in newspaper under his arm. He put it on the table while he went to get his cap from the hook on the kitchen door.

"What's that?" asked my mother. "Where you going?"

George picked up the parcel and put it under his arm. "I'm taking this up to Samuels. Pop it for bit. Get it out when something comes up."

"Can I come?" I asked, already scrambling for my shoes from under the dresser.

I loved the pawnbroker's. Mary, four years older, had acquired the dread and shame associated with its dealings by the grown-ups, but I had no such qualms.

Samuels was at the corner of the street. The three brass balls hanging outside announced its business and its shop windows were crammed with unredeemed pledges. Cousin George slunk like all the grown-ups round the corner to the discreet little side door and we stood in the conspiratorial semi-darkness of a cubicle, shielded from the inquisitiveness of other customers by its smooth mahogany walls.

"Lift me up," I said and George sat me on the wide mahogany counter. All around the walls were shelves stuffed with bundles of sheets, blankets and pillows. Overcoats and dresses of all shapes and sizes hung from the ceiling, each with a square cardboard ticket pinned to it with a huge safety pin.

Mr Samuels unwrapped the Taj Mahal. He looked up at Cousin George through thick steel-rimmed glasses. "Three pounds ten shillings for this lot, with the elephants."

"That'll do."

Now came the bit I had been looking forward to. Mr Samuels took hold of a pen and two more followed it. He placed three tickets on the counter and the pens, joined by metal rods, inscribed simultaneously the date, the amount pledged, and George's name. He tore the tickets apart, put one on a spike, one on George's parcel and handed the third over the counter.

George lifted me down and we made our way home.

"We'll call in at the sweetshop," he promised.

"What are you doing?" said Mum as we entered the door. "Sucking sweets just before your tea."

I gave Mary her bag of toffees and George handed my mother three pound-notes.

When Dad and brother John came in from work there was a bottle of lemonade and two pints of Guinness on the table. Mum took one shilling and ninepence from her purse. "Here, Mary. Go and get six pieces of cod and six pennorth of chips. You go with her, John, and fetch Dad a pint of brown. Take the blue jug."

John reached up for the jug and, sensing the mood, asked, "Can we have a game of cards tonight?"

Mary and I stayed up well after bedtime. For a while we lay listening to the fog horns sounding on the river. About nine-thirty, my father and Cousin George had retired to the pub and Mary and I giggled when we heard them return up the front passage.

George's fine strong tenor echoed up the stairs:

"God makes the bees, boys,
The bees make the honey–"
Dad joined in –
"The soldier does the dirty work
And the bookie takes the money!"

"Go on, George! Up you go before you wake the missus!"

Mary turned over in the bed, the evening's excitement leaving her restless.

"What did you do with that string of sugar?"
"Chucked it away."
"Oh ...."

The Taj Mahal never reappeared and to tell the truth it wasn't much missed.

Weeks later, George still hadn't had any 'luck'.

"Never mind," said Mum. "Keep smiling. Something'll turn up."

10

A Difficult Sum

It was almost the end of the school holidays and our hop-picking neighbours were expected back on Saturday. My mother considered hop-picking a notch below us in the league table of respectability so, much to my sorrow, we never took part in it.

Perhaps my mother couldn't stand watching my envious observation of the glorious disembarkation, with the children's cheeks like rosy apples shining through the dirt and big satisfied smiles on their faces. Even jumping down from the tailboard of a lorry was something out of the ordinary, after all. My mother maintained that, left on their own, the mattresses and blankets would jump down after them without assistance, but that meant nothing to me. Whatever the reason, the outing she had promised us instead took place that very day and threw in a drama that put even hopping in the shade.

On Saturday morning, my father went round our bedrooms like a sergeant major, hauling us out of bed by seven o'clock. As soon as we had finished breakfast, Mum took over.

"Get yourselves dressed while your father goes to fetch Aunt Alice," she commanded. "Mary, you can wear that new frock I altered for you, it's on the chair. Have you finished in the scullery, Ginny? John wants to come and have his wash."

She took the plimsoles down from the windowsill, where they'd been drying in yesterday's sun, and handed them to Mary and me. "Don't get these dirty before we go now. Your brother Blancoed them for you yesterday." She began to take the rags from Mary's hair with rapid little bird-pecking movements.

"Do you want curls, or don't you?" she demanded as Mary squealed.

Ginny joined us in the kitchen and began wrapping the two white cottage loaves, the cold sausages and apples for our picnic, stowing them into an oilcloth shopping bag. My mother produced a large currant cake from the cupboard beside the range and placed it on top.

"What we want now is the old kettle and the teapot, put the tea in it already and then all we have to do is wait for Aunt Alice."

She went upstairs to get herself ready and I followed Mary outside. With Mary's shiny black ringlets glistening in the sun in sharp contrast to my own straight fair bob, we stood on the doorstep to wait and to take the opportunity to show ourselves off to the street.

We watched them turn the corner from the main road, Aunt Alice a black, immobile figure sitting up in the great wicker bath chair, being pushed towards us by my father and a couple of urchins he had picked up on the way. He jammed on the brakes with a swift movement of his foot and ran up the steps.

"We're here, Nell," he called through the passage. "Bob's not so good, though. I've left the two girls with him."

My Uncle Bob had what was then commonly called consumption; a word which could have been used equally to describe the effect of TB on the individual patient and the effect it had on the density of population, and our family hadn't entirely escaped. It wasn't unknown for whole families to be wiped out in the 1920s and 1930s. The miracle was that, although in later years a medical examination revealed old TB lesions, I myself remained a healthy child, symptomless. All the more remarkable when you consider the fact that, before I reached school age, my contact with the disease could hardly have been closer because every day my mother would wheel me in a pushchair the half-mile or so to Uncle Bob's and Aunt Alice's house with their dinner wrapped in a white cloth, and not only did I jump up on Uncle Bob's bed for a cuddle, I even helped him eat his dinner, using the same spoon!

Aunt Alice though, we were told, was 'just' paralysed. How, I never found out. She was always our companion when we went on our family outings and, although I can't remember her saying so, I suppose it 'got her out of the house', as they say. Anyway, we soon set off, trundling the old wicker bath chair the three miles or so to Wimbledon Common, Mary and me as excited as though we were going to the moon. We followed the same route we had for years, my father monitoring our progress by calling encouragement each time we reached a familiar landmark.

The first lap took us through Kashmir Street and Delhi Place, two of the roughest places in the area. The old story that once the inhabitants had chopped up a copper and shoved him down a drain may have been myth, but the reality was grim enough. We moved as fast as we could past houses, some with sacks at the unglazed windows, some with missing front doors, their filth and squalor spilling out onto the pavement. A young-old woman, with hair the colour of dust, sat on a doorstep, breastfeeding a child of two or so. She pushed it away as we went past and it let out a whine.

"You have to wipe your feet on the mat before you step outside in some of these places," commented Dad as we walked past a tall paint-flaked hovel.

My mother made no response, glancing at the half-naked infant crawling in the dirt and quickly looking away again.

Ginny wrinkled up her nose. "Thank goodness the candle factory's at the top of the road. Smells like roses compared to this."

We turned into the main road, past the tenements we called the 'Dwellings' and the factories and warehouses that lined the river. A brewer's dray stood in the road while its load of wooden barrels was being lowered though a trapdoor to the pub on the corner and the big dray horse fed from a nosebag dripping with oats. While we waited for room to pass, the driver's boy carried a bucket of water from the pub for the horse to drink and the lid of the trapdoor was closed. The stale smell of last night's beer lingered in the air as we turned the corner into another world.

"Right!" shouted Dad. "Halfway there! Come on, John, your turn." He took off his cap and wiped his forehead. "Phew! It's a fair old weight and that bloody hill next!"

That 'bloody hill' was treelined, tram-free. Great detached houses, lawns neat and windows laundered, stood on both sides of the road. The sun was everywhere, patterning the pavement with tree shadows, painting the leaves bright with light. A lawnmower click-clicked in the garden beside us, sweetening the air with the aroma of newly-cut grass.

Now we all pushed, John and my father at the handle and the rest of us at the sides. At last, nearly at the top of the hill, my father stopped the chair and called as he always did, "First one to spot the winmill!" This time it was Mary.

"Winmill!" she yelled, and we caught a glimpse of the sail, gleaming white against a cloudless sky. As we grew nearer, the bright green grass edged by dark woods came into sight and we all pushed harder. I am sure that, even so long ago, there were the usual rules against lighting fires in the woods, but light one we did, and always had. In fact, it was done with such enthusiasm that it seemed almost as though the fire was the sole reason for the expedition. As far as Dad was concerned, I am sure it was.

"Get some smaller pieces!" he demanded as we ran around collecting timber. "No! That's too big. Right, give it to me! Where did I put the matches? Has Ginny come back from the winmill with the water yet?" And to John, "No. I'll put the match to it, just get out of the way. Wheel Aunt Alice round the other way, she'll have the smoke full in her face if you're not careful!"

My mother, unwrapping the food and spreading the tablecloth, looked on. "You sure it wasn't you who put a match to Madame Tussaud's the day it was burnt down?" she remarked acidly. She sat up on her knees while she held the loaf against her chest and sliced it with the knife towards her. "Do you want to eat now or have a play first?"

"Eat now!"

"I might have known."

She took the kettle from my father and poured water into it. "You've got time for one game of hiding seek."

After the picnic, we swung on the thick rope that my father hung onto the old oak and, waiting for my turn, I traced my finger along the familiar lines of its bark while Ginny swung up and up into the high leafy branches. We left the rope hanging while we played Leap Frog, Piggy in the Middle and, for my benefit, What's the Time, Mr Wolf?

Then came my father's favourite.

One exception to custom, and possibly the limit to our toleration of any sort of variation, was his game of Hunt the Something! With a show of extreme furtiveness and cunning, he would secretly hide an article from our baggage and challenge us to find it. Once it was the kettle itself and once, "Hey, not that, bring it back!" came from my mother as she saved her best black straw from his clutches. Being younger than the others and not so quick, I seldom found the cup or the teapot or the *Daily Herald* hidden in the bracken or a hole in a tree, but this day I *did* find something.

I think I had given up looking for whatever mysterious object Dad had stowed away somewhere, and the heavy scent of the late summer bracken and the unfamiliar silence broken only by the hum of insects was a rare opportunity to dream unnoticed and alone. What I was looking for in this secret world was no longer the lid of the teapot or an old envelope or the water bottle, but none other than the queen of the fairies or at least a smallish gnome. A favourite occupation this, pursued – it goes without saying – with absolute conviction.

The 'something' I did find though, impressed the others as much as if I'd got back to them trailing Titania herself. Running down the little footpath, I waved the rectangle of white paper over my head. "Is this it, Dad? I've found it. You hung it on a bush, didn't you?"

As my father took it from me, his face paled. He looked across at my mother and held the paper up to her with shaking hands.

"My God, Nell. It's a fiver!"

We were all silent. At last my mother spoke. "How d'you know?"

"I seen one before."

We spoke in whispers, "Show us, Dad, where does it say? Is it worth five pound notes? Did someone drop it?" He didn't answer but sat silently, occasionally exchanging long, serious looks with my mother, breathing fast.

It was almost all downhill on the way home. Tired out, I sat in the bath chair between Aunt Alice's feet and listened to my sisters as they fantasised over the big detached houses on the hill. Mary thought she'd have one of the gabled Victorian Villas when she got married.

"Old fashioned!" pooh-poohed Ginny.

As soon as we arrived home, my father went upstairs. We could hear him open the drawer of the wardrobe where all our Birth Certificates, mother's Marriage Lines and the Insurance Policies were stored. For the next six months, the piece of paper I had found was never mentioned and it stayed hidden in the wardrobe like a guilty secret shared. Then, just before Christmas, my father came in from the yard with a bucket of coal for the kitchen fire. He spoke to Mum as she got to her feet to lift the lid off the hob.

"Here, Nell," he said softly, "I've just thought of something."

"What?"

"Caffy. He'll change it."

She gave a grimace of fear.

"It'll be alright. After all this time. I'll take the littl'un with me to prove it."

Caffy was our local street bookie. It was some years before I learned that his real name was Cathwright. He was big and jolly and popular. In spite of his claim that half his takings went in police bribes, he used several houses in each street, in at the front and out through the back, in order to avoid being caught. It was a great source of excitement to us kids to see the bobbies after Caffy and to see him suddenly disappear into what seemed thin air. But as far as his punters were concerned, Caffy was honest in his dealings, willingly paying out on the highest odds and turning away nothing over a threepence each way bet. Everyone knew that, of course, in the end 'the only winner is the bookie' but, right or wrong, Caffy provided a little colour and excitement to the drab streets.

Caffy's runner, Charlie Fox, stood at the entrance to an alleyway, smoking a dark brown dog-end and occasionally taking a swift glance up and down the street. When we approached him, he took the cigarette from underneath his drooping moustache. He spoke in an habitual low monotone which wasn't quite a whisper. "Want a bet?"

"Nah, went down last week, had a tanner on the favourite. Where's Caff, Foxy?"

"Round the corner, up Mafeking. Go careful, they're out."

As we left him, I glanced back, but Foxy had vanished. We found Caffy in Mafeking Street, leaning up against the 'dead' wall, reading a newspaper. As we neared, he silently shook his head and went on reading.

"It's alright, Caff, I ain't got a bet."

Caffy put the newspaper down.

"What is it, Alf?"

"Can you change a fiver?"

Caffy straightened up and cast a quick look along the street.

"Where'd you get it?"

"The littl'un found it. Ages ago. She'll tell you." He pushed me towards the bookmaker.

"I found it when we went on the picnic. It was on a bush. When we had the school holidays."

Dad stared hard at Caffy. "What d'you think?"

"I'll see you in the Shakespeare. About eleven." He gave another swift glance up the street and was gone.

For the next four weeks, Mum was never 'out' when the rent man came and when Uncle Bob passed away three days before Christmas, the most splendid wreath of flowers at his funeral was signed, 'In deepest sympathy. With love, Nell, Alf and all the family'.

11

A Winter's Tale

Although the weather was bitingly cold, it didn't stop us children forsaking the warmth of the kitchen range for whatever exciting and interesting life was to be had in the street outside and, although what we witnessed would not usually be called adventure, it was intriguing enough for us.

There were five or six of us muffled against the weather in a sliding scale of effectiveness. The lucky ones (Miss Godwin's little Jenny and I were in this category) wore woollen stockings, coats and scarves. Jenny had a woollen bonnet and I wore a beret pulled down over my ears. Scarves were fitted round our middles and fastened at the back with safety pins. We were the only ones who wore gloves. In fact, what with woollen 'comms' (long underpants) and liberty bodices, we should have been as warm as toast, but we were both jumping up and down on the keystone in order to keep warm.

Dolly from over the road was not so well protected but as her dad ran a totting business she had managed to sort some rags out for herself before leaving her house and even sported a mangy bit of fur round her neck. As usual, her oversized drawers hung round her knees, so between those and her socks only a short length of bare leg was exposed to the elements.

The worst-off was Charlie Bunce who lived just short enough a distance round the corner of our street to still be included in our games. A few yards further away and he'd have been a foreigner. He was seated on the edge of the kerb in a pair of cut-down trousers reaching to his calves and a thin jersey with the elbows missing. When he stood up and went prancing down the road singing at the top of his voice, we could see the 'spuds' in the heels of his socks, like the scuds in a pair of fleeing rabbits.

Charlie was the oldest of a family of eight children who lived in two basement rooms. In spite of the burden of responsibility for his youngest brothers and sisters imposed upon him by his parents, he was one of the most cheerful of our group of playmates. He was always singing and at eleven, being older than most of us, up and about at all times. He could be heard in the street well after dark, carolling away in his piercing soprano, making my sister Mary and me giggle in our beds.

Charlie knew the words of each tune as soon as it came on the wireless. What is more, he was an instrumentalist, having somehow acquired a tin whistle and, because he picked up new tunes on first hearing, he was treated by us with the sort of admiration only previously accorded to the young Mozart. It turned out that, before the day was over, he would have given a mini star performance which impressed us even more.

The permanent channel of mucous that usually ran from his nose to his upper lip was now regularly transferred to the sleeve of his jumper as a gesture to polite convention. He had just paused in his rendering of *Every Time It Rains* in order to make this adjustment when Jackie Mills came down his front doorsteps and completed Charlie's song in his throaty street voice. Jackie had a tin can tied to a length of string which he swung round over his head. Wisps of smoke came from the holes in the can as he came to a halt at the edge of the kerb and held the can gingerly in his hands.

"Give us a go," said Doughnut, stamping his feet and hugging himself.

"Ere y'ar. It's blooming 'ot. There's a load of burning rags in it."

We all had a go, holding the can carefully so that it wouldn't burn our freezing fingers, and in spite of Jackie's swinging of the string in order to liven it up, the fire inside the tin soon died. "That was a good'un, wasn't it?" said Jackie, opening the tin and examining the rags for signs of life.

We all agreed. We stared at each other for a time, each of us deciding to find a tin as soon as we went back home, when Dolly announced out of the blue: "My cousin Jimmy's got the fever." The 'fever' was usually diphtheria, sometimes scarlet fever, which I had been fortunate enough to survive. Often a killer in those days, these were two of the major illnesses that constantly threatened our community. They were taken seriously as potential catastrophes and treated with respect.

The endless list of minor illnesses that beset us were taken for granted as normal. Impetigo, boils, quinsies, bad teeth and crossed eyes were so common that a group of children could easily be mistaken for a bunch of medieval peasants out on the spree.

Our family didn't escape all of these. Certainly we avoided impetigo, kept at bay by my mother's paranoid cleanliness. The universal scourge though, during these winter months, was chilblains. At school we scratched, itched and fidgeted our way through lessons in inadequately heated classrooms, were tormented to screaming pitch at mealtimes and with feet swollen and nerves torn to shreds we would fret ourselves to sleep, exhausted.

Woolworths did a roaring trade in an ointment in a little tin labelled 'Snowfire'. Whether it helped or not, I can't remember; certainly, the name was appropriate.

Immersing the affected parts in a full chamber pot was a remedy enthusiastically recommended by some of our neighbours but my mother was too fastidious to put it to the test, so we continued tormented until adulthood, with fur-lined boots, carpeted floors and central heating.

We listened carefully to Dolly's news, although her cousin Jimmy was unknown to us. We shared with the grown-ups a lively interest in these catastrophes which were constant topics of gossip and conversation. We stood in the cold wind while Dolly searched through her mind for embellishments. "He didn't go to the fever hospital in the daytime, you know," she boasted, pulling her bit of rabbit fur closer round her neck. "The amberlance came in the middle of the night. My mum says red roar, his froat was. 'E's only six. My mum didn't 'arf cry."

We were silent for a while, digesting this bit of minor sensationalism and wishing we had a similar tale to tell. Nothing came up though and we warmed ourselves up with a brisk game of 'He' until another half-dozen or so joined us and Syddy Rolls went in to fetch a tin can for a game of 'Tin Can Copper'.

This was a favourite game and in no time someone had kicked the can down the middle of the road and Doughnut stood still with his eyes tightly closed. The rest of us ran away, hiding in doorways, down area steps and up alleyways. No place was sacrosanct and the noise must have driven the grown-ups mad. Doughnut opened his eyes, caught a glimpse of Syddy peering from a doorway and bawled, "I see Syddy Rolls!" He banged the can on the ground with a "One two three!" As he put the can on the ground several others rushed to kick it away again and thus release Syd, the usual heated argument ensued and the noise reached crescendo heights.

"Clear off down your own end of the street!" Old Mother Budd, a thin lady of at least thirty came out onto her doorstep brandishing a wet mop. As we were a crowd of kids from every part of the street – including Charlie from round the corner – this proved a tall order. However, we made a token move to a few yards away from the Budds' house and continued our game. This took our base to number twenty-seven, where Old Coalie kept his sacks of coal in the basement and supplied all the street with small quantities of coal and coke. Today his basement window was quiet and dark, with the curtains drawn, his little coal trucks standing empty in rows inside the area. We never gave this a thought.

If you weren't afraid of Old Coalie you had to pretend to be or be thought a spoilsport. Charlie alone got away with his scornful, "Yah! I ain't afraid of Coalie. Can't hurt yer!" because he was older than most of us and considered getting on for being grown-up.

We didn't notice anything strange about Coalie's being shut on a day when the weather would have encouraged a more than usual trade in bags of fuel and it wasn't until later on the same day when I heard my mother talking to Miss Godwin about him that I remembered the quiet windows and drawn curtains.

"Never talks to a soul, you know. Not even to Mrs Jackson who lives upstairs in the house. She thinks he's gone away again. He did before. Came back after a week without a word to say where he'd been or anything. We had to take the pushchair round to Pendegrass's to get our bag of coke this week. One thing, he'll be warm enough with all that coal!"

'Tin Can Copper' kept us busy until dinnertime and when Jenny and I emerged onto the front doorstep, muffled to the ears once again, we were stopped short by the sight that met our eyes. We immediately turned on our tracks, pulled the string on the door and rushed in.

"It's snowing! It's snowing!"

Mum came out, a pleased smile on her face. "It's pretty," she said.

The fall was thick and fast; in a few minutes it had obliterated the grey roofs, broken fences and lined the window frames with white lace. The flakes flew almost horizontally, massing against walls, kerbs and lampposts in great drifts, softening off edges and angles until there wasn't a straight line to be seen.

Within seconds, every door in the street had opened. Children came tumbling out to pay their ecstatic respect to the benign visitation, blinking their eyes in the new brightness and pulling on whatever outdoor garments they could muster. The thrill of seeing our footprints, the first in the snow on the steps, the snowball fights and the big snowball rolled up against the alley wall kept us busy for an hour or more until raw frozen fingers and soaking wet feet drove us inside. Jenny, Mary and I stamped ourselves dry on the front porch and sat thankfully beside the kitchen stove, whimpering with pain as the blood slowly returned to our hands and feet.

We heard the factory hooters signal five-thirty and a few minutes after that my father came in from work. He nodded to Miss Godwin, "They can keep this bloody stuff!" He shook the surplus snow from his coat in the scullery sink but didn't take his boots off as usual. "Three blokes off today, Jack's got pleurisy and Nobby Clark's Mrs came in to say he's got pains in the chest. Won't go to the doctor. The governor told her he'll have to if he wants a certificate for being off work. We're working like blooming slaves up there."

"I saw Mrs Jackson on my way down the street," he continued. "She wants me and young Ginger Salmon to get into Coalie's tonight. Reckons she heard something down there. I'll go and get Ginger and have my tea after."

My father was gone for quite a time and we had our tea and dressed to savour the feel of playing in the snow by the light of the streetlamps.

Charlie Bunce and Syddy and a little group of others were out there when we arrived in the street. There was no sign of my father or Ginger-Nut. Then Syddy pointed up the road. An ambulance was squelching its way through the slush to stop at Coalie's house. We rushed over to it and several women came out to stand on the pavement by it. After a while, Coalie's basement door opened and my father stood there. Two ambulance men disappeared inside and the little crowd on the pavement grew larger. The women, some with men's caps on their heads or with scarves to keep out the cold, chattered excitedly.

We stood expectantly until the ambulance men, my father and Ginger came out from the basement door carrying Coalie's large figure covered in a red blanket on a stretcher. The slope of the area steps was precarious and the stretcher in danger of losing its contents, so there was a great deal of heaving and grunting. Before they reached the top of the steps, the snowflakes stood out white against the red blanket.

The group of watchers grew silent as the stretcher reached the pavement. It was then that Charlie disappeared. He ran like lightning to his house and returned in a minute with his tin whistle. My father and Ginger stood aside and the ambulance men made ready to slide the stretcher and its burden into the open doors of the ambulance. Now a single plaintive note was carried through the cold air and Charlie, standing as straight as a die, followed it with what he considered a fitting tribute to the occasion. Following his example, we kids drew ourselves up, raised our right hands in a salute to our foreheads and sang to his accompaniment:

"God Save Our Gracious King.
Long live our Gracious King.
God Save our King."

The women looked on in astonishment. I saw my father put his hand to his moustache to hide a grin. The doors of the ambulance slammed shut and it was all over.

As my father sat at the table eating his tea, my mother looked on. "They said he'd be alright, then? Just collapsed with cold? Are you certain about the grate?"

"Oh yes, Nell. You ask Ginger. Never had a fire in it for years."

12

The R100

The choice between exciting street games with dozens of other children readily available from dawn to dusk is a luxury no longer afforded to today's children.

Traffic was confined to a few horses and carts and the occasional delivery van. We had our bread delivered by a small and very elegant-looking pony and trap. The driver was smart, too – I think he was the owner of the bakery – and his flat cloth cap, whip and bright leather leggings stood out in striking contrast to most people round our way. These few vehicles and the rare event of a motor bike and sidecar allowed for plenty of safety in our streets.

On this particular day, Mary and I chose not to play in the street. My mother and her friend (Mrs Jaw-me-dead to my father) were in the scullery discussing the many and varied shortcomings of Mr J. There seemed to be some competition in this dialogue, my mother having first shot with Dad's misdemeanours and Mrs J topping the score.

We were quite familiar with this little exchange

and, being pretty sure that there was nothing new to be overheard, Mary and I went out to play in the back yard. Mary took a piece of chalk from the pocket of her pinny and wrote 2+2 on the lavatory door.

"I'm teacher," she announced, "what's the answer?"

"Five."

"Come out here and stand with your back to the class!"

I did so, putting my tongue out and crossing my eyes. Mary, so often landed with the chore of looking after me, seldom succeeded in getting something out of it for herself but being teacher was some compensation.

Mrs J's visit didn't last long. Meanwhile, we changed over to playing four-stones on the back doorstep. Mary was an expert and I had always admired the deftness of her fingers as she threw the coloured stone cubes into the air and palmed the little rubber ball in a smooth, continuous rhythm.

While we played, we could hear my mother stoking up the stone copper, our hot water system. She carried the big zinc bucket to the shallow sink half a dozen times, filled the metal-lined bowl inside the copper and replaced the wooden lid. She did this twice a week, once on washdays and again on Saturdays for our weekly baths.

As the water began to boil, we could smell the hot, soapy steam and hear the water bubbling.

Soon the copperstick would be used to heave the steaming white sheets and drop them into the rinsing water in the big zinc bath. A second lot of water would be ready to give them another rinse in Reckitt's Blue before the mangling. But Mum hadn't reached that stage yet and we could hear her refuelling the fire through the little aperture down near the floor.

After a while she called out, "I'm closing the door, you two, so mind out."

"Why?"

"Oh, I don't know. It's cold in here."

We shifted off the step and chalked a rough hopscotch plan over the uneven bricks of the yard floor and, after a couple of skips over them, returned to the doorstep.

"Let's go out to play," said Mary, and pushed open the scullery door.

There was a shout. "Shut that door at once!"

Mum stood facing us, face rigid, her apron spread out in front of the copper, her legs apart. And then, too late, we saw him, nearly all gone, only his old head, one eye missing and no ears, poking out of the copper.

"Teddy Big! My lovely Teddy Big!" howled Mary at the top of her voice.

Mum stood holding her breath, her face, already red from her furtive and hurried exertions, growing redder.

"Stop that noise! You haven't even looked at him for years. He's been under all that junk in the cupboard, ever since you were five! Now, hold your noise, do you hear me?" She hustled us towards the front door. "Go out to play." She gave me a shove, "You too."

Once outside, Mary seemed to get over her loss pretty quickly, and was soon wrapping herself round a lamppost, swinging from a hemp rope, while I stood and watched the big boys racing their scooters up and down the middle of the road. The din they made was deafening. They were wooden homemade scooters with ball-bearings for wheels and the owner's number proudly displayed on the upright at the front, racing along with shouts of "Come on number seven!", etc, echoing up and down the street.

An adult voice cut through the yelling. Mr Dobbs, the old bachelor who was the lodger at number six, was leaning out of an upstairs window and looking up at the sky.

We all threw back our heads and gazed upwards. Old Dobbs gesticulated with the stem of his pipe, nearly falling out of the window in his excitement. We rushed up the front steps and pulled the string that worked the latch inside, falling over each other in our eagerness to see what was in the sky. Mum came to meet us from the kitchen, her sleeves rolled up past the elbows and her arms covered with soapsuds.

"Whatever's the matter?" she cried.

"There's something up in the sky!"

We pushed past her and rushed into the back yard. For a few minutes we searched the sky and then, over to the north of the city, saw a huge cigar-shaped object just coming into view. Although the air currents seemed to lift it and shift it as easily as if it were a child's balloon, it still moved with a silent, grave majesty.

Mum grabbed the ladder and held it while we climbed onto the shed roof. We watched it spellbound as it turned its side towards us.

"R100," Mary read out from the great black letters painted on the side.

"It's the biggest thing I've ever seen. Bigger than all the airplanes in the world put together," I cried.

As it slowly disappeared over the rooftops, glinting silver in the sudden sunshine, Mum lifted us down from the shed.

"Would you believe there are people in it?" she asked. "Tables and chairs, a posh restaurant all laid out with starched tablecloths and real silver knives and forks, with waiters, and everyone all dressed up to the nines?"

"Like on the pictures?" Mary asked.

"That's right. Like on the pictures."

"Wish we could have a ride in it. Could we?"

"Shouldn't think so. Unless my ship comes in."

"Who's in it, then?"

"Oh, I dunno. Lord and Lady Dunabunk, I expect. Rich people, anyway. Come on, I've got two-dozen whites to finish for Mrs Charlton. You can help me with the mangling."

Later on, out in the street, people were still standing around stringing out the experience of the first airship they'd seen or spinning yarns about the German Zeps that raided London a decade before, and we kids played around, half listening to the talk.

At six o'clock my father turned the corner at the top of the road. He carried his lunch tin in his hand and had taken off his jacket. As we reached him, he took off his cap and wiped his forehead.

"Phew! It's turned hot all of a sudden."

He moved towards the house with us clinging to his arms.

"Dad!" said Mary. "Guess what happened today."

"Yeah. I saw it," he said, "the R100..."

"No! Not that!" She put herself in front of him, blocking his way into the house, and tears came into her eyes.

"Mum burnt Teddy Big!"

13

Problems

Something strange happened round about this time. Something that I never fully understood until I was an adult and had a family of my own.

It was a day when everything had gone wrong at school, starting with the arithmetic lesson. I was then – and still am – almost completely innumerate. Numbers flit in and out of my head like swallows in flight and that morning we were being given what Miss Spence called a 'little test'. For me, a 'little test' in arithmetic evoked the same dread and panic as would a 'little drowning' or a 'little strangulation', so I stared glassy-eyed at Miss Spence as she stood, in front of our rows of raked desks, looking over the top of her gold-rimmed spectacles.

She was a Scot, although at the time we didn't know it, only that she talked funny. She was small and neat and had thin grey hair that was scraped up into a bun on top of her head. When she said the word 'arithmetic' she rolled the 'r' with an emphasis that could only be called menacing, as though the word itself wasn't enough to put the fear of God in me already.

"Take out your books and turn to page 9," she ordered.

With my heart in my boots, I stared out of the window, where the tip of the great crane on the dockside soared away into the blue.

"Did you hear me, girl, or are you still in bed and sleeping?" (A small titter from the rest of the class.)

I took out the book and turned to page nine while Miss Spence took the blackboard rubber and erased the writing from the easel. She had to reach up and we caught a glimpse of the bottom of her cotton petticoat beneath her grey wool skirt.

With a piece of white chalk she wrote '15th April 1932' in her large careful handwriting and underneath that 'PROBLEMS. Page 9.'

There was a knock at the classroom door and a girl's face appeared at the glass panel.

"Come in!" commanded Miss Spence irritably and two monitors entered the room carrying a metal crate of forty milk bottles, each containing one third of a pint. The monitors slid the crate noisily under the radiator and left.

I gazed at the closed door for a moment, willing someone else to knock: for the headmistress to come with some special announcement; for the milk monitor to return because someone hadn't paid their halfpenny for their milk or, better still, for the Fire Drill bell to ring. None of these things happened and I took the pen from the groove in the desk, dipped it in the inkwell and dutifully repeated '15th April 1932, Problems. Page 9.'

I opened the textbook. Problem No 1:

'Two boys and their father were picking apples in an orchard. The father had picked ten pounds, the biggest boy five pounds and the youngest two and a half pounds. How many more apples would the boys have to pick to make the total of apples into twenty pounds?

My eyes wandered to the window and out to the tip of the crane, yellow against the cloudless sky.

A ruddy-faced, cheerful-looking man in a round brimmed hat, a white smock and leather gaiters, stood on a ladder propped against a tree. He carried a large canvas bag over his shoulder and was dropping big rosy apples into it, one by one.

Perched on the ladder just below him was a big lad in a Norfolk jacket and knee breeches, smiling up at his father and reaching for the nearest fruit, while down below on the ground a little fellow in a sailor suit and a big Panama hat scrabbled on the ground for windfalls. A white cat lay nearby, dozing in the sun and a blackbird trilled its notes from the other side of the orchard.

There was a sudden jab in the small of my back.

"You have not even started. You will stay in at four o'clock until you finish and until you have done them correctly! Start now, this minute, do you understand?"

I felt her sharp blue eyes piercing the back of my head.

'Apples', I wrote in a state of near panic. She left me and underneath I wrote '$5 + 2\% = 7\%$.'

Problem No.2 was about a tank of water which

for some reason or other was taking in gallons of water and letting it out at the bottom. The big zinc grey tank with bolts all over it and rust streaking its sides held very little interest for me and after reading the question two or three times and making not much of it, I left it out.

I glanced sideways at Margery, my desk companion, and she hastily hid her work behind her sleeve. I felt a faint consolation that she had a big hole under her arm revealing her grubby vest.

Problem 3 involved two trains travelling at different speeds between London and Cambridge. I had never been to Cambridge but knew that it sported a pale blue colour on Boat Race Day and that I always wore its favour and once had even cheered it on from Putney Bridge. The two trains chuffed along, trailing their plumes of white steam. A boy leaned out of a window, waving to passers-by on top of the embankment. Then the slower engine started to gain speed. It grew nearer the leading train. There was an almighty crash. Coaches lay overturned. Luggage was strewn over the track. Residents from nearby houses were tearing up sheets to bind the wounds of screaming victims.

Miss Spence's icicle-sharp voice cut through the scene.

"Right! Put your pens down now. Collect the books, monitors."

Margery put her pen in the groove of her desk. Her book was still open. 'Train No.2', I read at the bottom of the page. It took me a second or so to scrawl the same answer in my book and with a smile of relief hand it to the monitor. Then the bell went, signalling the end of the morning, and it was all over. Time to head home for dinner.

Dinnertime was a scratch affair on Mondays. The scullery and kitchen were full of steam from the stone copper and everything smelled of soap. My mother placed the plate of cold meat and mashed potatoes on the kitchen table, her hands and arms red from the soft, soapy water and went back into the scullery to continue her work. When I had finished eating I disappeared into the lavatory at the end of the garden where I sat dreaming that I had swum the Channel and on leaving the beach had been proposed to by a famous film star.

When I got back to the kitchen I found that my mother wasn't alone. A young lad in a thick grey tweed suit and a brand-new grey cap in his hand was standing at the kitchen door. His straight black hair, shiny with brilliantine, had been recently cut and was parted neatly on one side. His shoes gleamed with newness.

He gave my mother a nervous half-smile and spoke in a soft voice with an accent strange to me.

"So you don't know where she could have gone from here, or anyone around here who might know my mother?"

Mum shook her head.

"I've got an hour or two left to look for her. We don't sail until tonight and as I'm down here I thought I'd try to get in touch." He stood in silence for a moment, twisting his cap round and round in his hands. My mother made no reply, continuing to shake her head.

"Never had the chance before, being up north," he continued. "I'm a Barnado's boy, you see, and I'm now off to Australia." He held out a piece of paper. "They gave me this address for her –" he moved his head slowly from side to side, searching my mother's face – "you're sure you can't help me?"

My mother finished wiping her hands on her apron and held them up in a helpless gesture. She looked him straight in the eyes. "I am sorry, lad. She went a long way away, that I do know, right out of London, but where, I've no idea. I wish I could tell you."

The boy turned towards the door. My mother followed him into the passage and held the front door open for him. "Good luck, son." She closed the door.

"Who was that?" I demanded. "Who was he looking for?"

She retreated into the scullery. "Mind your own business. It's time you went back to school." Her voice sounded strange and I hesitated, standing by the kitchen table. There was a slip of paper on it. 'Miss C. Godwin', I read. 'Last known address…'

"Mum!" I called, "He's forgotten this."

I showed it to her as she came quickly through from the scullery.

She snatched it from my hand. "You are going to

be late!" She screwed the paper up and put it into her apron pocket. "Get off now!"

I thought about it all the way to school. 'Miss C. Godwin. Last known address...'

If it were she the boy was looking for, if Miss Godwin was his mum, then my mother had told him a lie. Miss Godwin was less than a quarter of a mile away, round at Belcher's. If he had come from the station he would have passed her, serving fish at the counter! I couldn't make it out but by the time I arrived at school I had relegated it to one of the many aspects of adult behaviour that was both mysterious and ambiguous.

We had cookery lesson in the afternoon. That morning, we had each brought a small dish and an egg from home. There were always a few who came without them of course and after being subject to a five-minute nagging from Miss Guest, the cookery teacher, were 'loaned' the ingredients from her store. Miss Guest was about fifty with a mass of auburn hair tucked under a white cap. She ran everywhere, talking all the time, nudging and pushing us into our places at the tables, the sink and the oven.

"Right! Hands first!" She herded a group of us to the wash basins, turned on the taps, grabbed the hands of the nearest girl, and forced the soap into them. "A good scrub, now. Nails as well. I shall want to see them when you have finished! Aprons and caps next!"

We had hardly time to wash before she took a

few steps backward and rushed at us, pushed us over to where the aprons and caps hung on a row of hooks, snatched them off the wall and threw them towards us.

"Hurry now! Haven't got all day."

Like a whirlwind she dashed around tying the tapes that fastened the aprons all down the back and stuffing as many of the caps as she could onto our heads. I stood at my place by the long, scrubbed table in a daze, cap on head and my apron reaching to my feet. A girl gave out forks and we proceeded to imitate Miss Guest's demonstration of egg-beating. If all cooks had been like Miss Guest, the mechanical egg-beater would never had been invented. Holding her hands high, she whirled her fork until we could see neither hand nor wrist. Finished in seconds, she rushed us off to the next stage.

"Come on. Line up here. A quarter of a pint each onto your beaten egg."

We poured the milk onto our half-beaten eggs and sprinkled sugar on the top. Miss Guest had the dishes in the oven in a trice and we sat at our desks in the corner to write the recipe. The sheet of lined white paper she had placed in front of each of us reminded me of my task at four o'clock after school and I felt a stab of apprehension. It eased a little as Miss Guest grabbed the pen and thrust it into my hand, saying, "Come on now, girl! You are my best writer. Get on. We haven't got all day!"

When the dishes came out of the oven it was

time to clean up. Miss Guest whirled around, distributing sackcloth aprons, buckets, and scrubbing brushes. We spent the next ten minutes scrubbing the already pristine table using what she called 'elbow grease'. Two girls were allocated the job of cleaning the floor, Miss Guest chasing after them in an impatient trot and our lesson was over.

Our next task was to carefully carry home the results of our labour and for some of us it was quite a hazardous task. Predators in the form of boys lurked outside the cookery room which was in their playground, waiting for us to emerge. They hid in the outside lavatory, behind coal bins and in doorways, grinning and rolling their eyes in anticipation of fun to come.

The problem for the would-be cooks was how to get to the door in the wall that led to our own school without spilling the contents of our bowls before the boys caught up with us. Some of us sometimes made it. This time I didn't. Billy Baxter, thirteen and zealous in his aggressive courtship of the girls, popped out from behind a dustbin and, with one sweep of his hand, tipped up egg custard all over my frock and shoes. He ran and I screamed, bringing Miss Guest out of the cookery classroom and onto the step. She took me inside and with a brisk rub of a wet towel had me cleaned up in a second.

"And who was the little devil who did this?" she demanded briskly.

I told her. I wasn't too put off by Billy's attentions

usually, when it just meant being chased and thrown to the ground or held prisoner up against a brick wall for a time and I often gave as good as I got, but there was no sense of loyalty between us that prevented me from 'telling on him'.

The church clock struck a quarter past four as I left the classroom and, reminded of my tryst with the arithmetic problems, with a sinking heart hurried through the door that led to the girls' school. When I reached the classroom, however, it was empty. The desks were cleared. Miss Spence's chair was on her table ready for the cleaners and Miss Spence was nowhere to be seen. The incident with the egg custard had made me too late. I heaved a sigh of relief. Things wouldn't end there, but tomorrow was another day and I wandered home, this time unmolested, with the remains of my egg custard.

Pushing school and its problems aside for a time, I lay in bed that night and thought about the boy who had come to our house at dinnertime. Why hadn't Mum given him a cup of tea or even some dinner? It wasn't like her. It seemed she couldn't get rid of him quickly enough. And what were all these fibs about Miss Godwin living a long way away? I knew they were questions I didn't dare ask and fell asleep none the wiser.

14

Missing

We didn't see much of Miss Godwin after she went to live at Bill Belcher's. My mother never visited her there and it was only when we were up at the High Street to buy fish from Belcher's that my mother would stand talking to her as she served on the open shop front.

Miss Godwin seemed to have shrunk. Never very tall, she nevertheless had once had a plump healthy roundness, which had given way to an unattractive skinnyness.

She wore an old brown oilskin apron, once belonging to Belcher, her down-at-heel shoes slopped around in a stream of water and as she handled the fish from the icy slabs we could see the little nicks and cuts in her fingers running with blood.

My mother's indignation knew no bounds.

"Her hands are raw, blue with the cold. She looks as though she could do with a good meal, too. He hasn't served in the shop since she got there," she'd complain.

"She's made her bed, gal," was Dad's regular response.

Little Jenny was three, though, before real troubles came.

My friend Bella and I were in the back yard putting the finishing touches to our guy. We were engaged in a truly co-operative effort. Bella had borrowed her dad's box cart and we were to construct the top half of the guy. Because the Rollses had a pair of old trousers they were responsible for the bottom half. We were busily stuffing the sleeves of the coat with straw when we heard the sudden commotion and ran into the kitchen to see what was up.

Jenny was sitting on Dad's lap yelling blue murder while Miss Godwin, her face black with bruises, sobbed in my mother's arms.

This was no place for us.

"Here, you two, off you go out, and take Jenny with you. Look after her. Don't go far." Mum bundled us out, guy and all.

Outside, the weather was damp and raw. The air was thickening with the promise of a real London pea-souper and, before we set out, we stopped and sat on the doorstep to fasten all the buttons on Jenny's gaiters and wind the woollen scarf round her body to be tied at the back.

Stuffing Jackie's and Dolly's contribution into the lower half of the cart, we made for the railway arch. It was now early afternoon and the air was growing even colder in the thick yellow mist as it closed in around us. Passers-by, hands in their pockets and faces hidden in turned-up collars, walked quickly towards the shelter of their homes and rarely responded to our "Penny for the guy, Mister."

We stayed at it for half an hour or so.

"I'm going home," complained Bella as she rubbed the chilblains that glowed through the holes in the heels of her socks. "I'm frozen."

"We've only got tuppence." For the umpteenth time Dolly Rolls adjusted the cardboard face on the head of the guy. "Look, his face keeps falling off. You didn't make the top half big enough, that's why."

Jackie, even more glum, announced, "It's a rotten guy."

Bella and I turned on him.

"You and Dolly made the bottom half too big. You should have got littler trousers."

"And your half's a kid's coat. So it's your fault if it's all wrong." He wound himself up into a defiant conclusion. "Me and Dolly ought to have the tuppence!"

Bella and I stared in shock dismay.

"It's my cart!" shouted Bella.

"And this is my 'alf," responded Jackie, as he hauled out the bottom part of the guy and draped it round his neck, a leg over each shoulder. "Come on, Doll, hold his stuffing in."

We watched him march away, dissolving into the thickening fog with Dolly behind him doing her best to keep the straw from escaping.

After a minute he was back, still with Dolly running at his heels. He threw a penny into the cart. "'Ere y'ar." He was as aware as we all were that all hell can be let loose where dispute involving as much as a penny was concerned. The grown-ups would be brought in for a start.

As he retreated, Bella and I looked woefully at the remains of our handiwork, now collapsed in a heap at the bottom of the cart.

"He looks boozed," giggled Bella. "Come on, let's go home. We can give Jenny a ride."

But Jenny, when we went to pick her up, wasn't there. We stared into the fog.

"She was there just now," I said, suddenly terrified.

"She still is," consoled Bella. "Can't see her, that's all."

The other end of the railway arch was now invisible. We shouted and screamed Jenny's name, ran up and down the pavement and backwards and forwards across the road, appealing to the dwindling numbers of passers-by. Then, finally, in a panic, we made for home.

We pushed the cart through the sulphurous green mist, scarcely finding our way. At every shop, the yellow gas light from its windows barely penetrating to the pavement and its front door tightly closed, we stopped to ask for her.

We were both sobbing with anxiety when Jenny suddenly materialised out of the gloom. There she was, outside the rag-a-bone shop, the fog swirling round her, sitting in an old wooden highchair, marked '2/6d', blissfully gnawing on the biggest toffee apple we'd ever seen and watched from the shop door by old Rag-Bone himself.

"She yourn?" He lifted her down. "Take her home and hold onto her this time."

When we reached our house, Miss Godwin had gone back to the shop and Mum, after standing her up in a basin of water on the table to wash some of the stickiness off, took Jenny to her.

She seemed pretty pre-occupied that evening, so there didn't seem much point in telling her all about the mislaying of Jenny.

15

A Moving Experience

"Guess what?"

My sister Mary climbed into bed beside me and gave her usual tug at the bedclothes, leaving my right leg exposed to the chilly air of the bedroom. I heaved them back.

"What?"

"We're moving."

"Where to?" I felt a spasm of fear in my stomach and clutched at Mary's nightdress.

"We're getting a council house. The council's coming next Tuesday. Mum's had a letter. It's going to be brand new with an indoor lav an' all."

"Who said?"

"Mum. The letter's just come. Last post."

"Don't believe you." A stock denial in response to information handed down. I did though, and didn't much like it.

There was an air of jubilation at breakfast the next morning. Mum stood at the kitchen table, staring across at my father with a contented smile on her face. She held the big cottage loaf against her apron and was carving slices of crusty white bread. "Well, we've waited long enough, eh Alf?" She stood up and leaned over to place a slice on my brother John's plate.

"Yea, about time. You've wrote often enough. Get us away from that lot downstairs".

'That lot downstairs' were the Trotts, a family of two adults and seven dirty and neglected children living in our two basement rooms. Mrs Trott had come to the house seeking rooms five years before, with two babies in an old pram and a depressed-looking husband with a drooping moustache and droopier shoulders. Why my parents sublet to them we never discovered. My mother was never a good manager with money, and you needed to be, what with Dad earning under three pounds a week, which was on the low side even for 1928. Maybe they were hard up, although it was just as likely that they took pity on the scruffy couple. Whatever the reason, they paid dearly for it.

Mrs Trott was a woman in her thirties, cross-eyed and almost toothless; she looked ancient. Several times a day, we would be treated to her appearance in our kitchen when she came through to fetch water from the house's only tap in the scullery, her old beaten-down boots shuffling along the lino, the hem of her filthy skirt trailing. If my mother had a visitor, Mrs Trott was sure to appear.

And each time, my fastidious mother would draw in her breath and turn her head away.

Mary and I grew used to the Trotts and scarcely noticed the clamour and cries of hungry children that created a background to our lives, or the smell of ammonia that pervaded the staircases and reached to the bedrooms, the fleas hopping up the basement steps. But as my parents and Ginny and John, our elder brother and sister, constantly complained, it became routine and the Trotts grew to be a part of home life that didn't disturb us younger ones.

On this morning, though, because Mum got up earlier than usual and we followed her downstairs so there was plenty of time before school and work, and because everyone was so excited –and perhaps also because we were going to leave the Trotts for ever – Mary and I added our comments to the long diatribe of charges against our sub-tenants.

"Don't know what they do with the water she comes to get," said brother John, munching on his bread and jam. "Reckon she pours it away when she gets downstairs."

"Nobody will sit with them in school, they're so dirty," added Mary.

"They always get three for fleas when Nitty Nora comes," I chimed in.

"Well, you just keep away from them," ordered my mother.

The segregation in the house was complete, although we saw plenty of the younger Trotts, with their bare feet and bare bottoms, playing on the area steps.

The rest of the day's topics took in similar derogatory accusations concerning the neglect of the Trott children, the failure of Mr Trott to pay the three-and-sixpence a week for rent and the regular yearly appearance of new little Trotts.

In between, we speculated on the probable location of the new house and how near or far it might be to school and work.

"I don't care where it is," announced Mum. "Timbuctoo'll do!"

Ginny butted in eagerly, "Perhaps it'll be where Mary Thomas lives. She's moved into a council house. It's got a scullery with a bath in it with hot water coming out of the taps and a board over the top and it's all brand new with a green front door and a garden in the front as well as the back. It's not with a row of other houses, there are just two together with a space between the next two. They've got three bedrooms in theirs but I expect we'll get four."

She walked over to the mirror and smiled complacently at herself.

My mother spent Monday afternoon looking through her old servant's trunk from her days in service; here she kept odds and ends of discarded curtaining.

"Some of this'll do, Ginny," she announced in the evening, holding up a length of check gingham to my sister, "or shall we have all new?"

That evening, we all went to tell Aunt Alice who lived on her own and had been an invalid for as long as I could remember. She lived in a little double-fronted house, built before the railway, with a tiny triangle of a yard cut to size and shape by the line from Clapham Junction. The railway bank rose steeply from the railings at the back of the house on which Michaelmas Daisies, Rosebay Willow Herb and Dog Daisies grew in profusion. My mother loved that house and one summer had prised apart one of the tall iron railings that separated the yard from the bank and squeezed through to lay out a tiny plot of a garden planted with seeds from a penny packet. When summer came she wheeled Aunt Alice out to see the little row of nasturtiums and white daisies growing among the Sweet William.

On the other side of the house there were French windows, long fastened up and opening on to nothing but nevertheless retaining some of the elegance that once may have been, long ago before the railway came when the little house stood in its own grounds.

Standing at the end of a cul-de-sac of old London cottages, two up and two down, with tumbledown wooden fences and crumbling window frames, the wide sky over the embankment and the quiet broken only by the soft *chuff-chuff* of the shunting engines in the distance, it was a shade quieter and brighter and, in comparison with its surroundings, almost rural. Alice knew my mother's love for the house and had already persuaded its owner to allow our family to live in it 'if anything happened to her', but nobody spoke of that and the general consensus was that it was falling to bits anyway. But then, so was everywhere else.

Alice called my mother her lifeline. Each day at twelve-thirty Mum would start out for Aunt Alice's, walking through the grey streets with their dirty pavements and drab houses, pushing a pushchair containing Alice's dinner. She had been doing this for as long as I could remember. In fact, in my first memories of it, I was a pushchair passenger clutching the plates wrapped in a cloth on my knees.

"Can't stay long, Alice," she'd say, pushing the bath chair up to the table, taking the white cover off the plate and laying out the knife and fork, "got to get back to give the two girls their dinner. They'll be out of school and waiting for me by now."

So naturally, the old lady was upset by the news about the move. "Don't worry, Alice," comforted Mum, full of optimism about the possibilities inherent in her new life, "we shall see just as much of you. It's bound to be in the Borough."

Mary and I left our elders talking animatedly in Aunt Alice's kitchen and went through the scullery into the little yard. An engine, invisible on the other side of the embankment, chugged its way past and a plume of white steam streaked the blue sky. We sat on the concrete with our legs thrust through the railings onto Mum's garden patch.

"Our new house'll have a proper garden, you know, grass and flowers. P'raps trees," Mary spoke with the authority of an older sister.

"No it won't." My response was automatic, while my imagination conjured up Kew Gardens. "There might be bushes," I conceded.

That night we were in bed late. Lino that had already been scrubbed to annihilation was scrubbed again. Cupboards were turned out, windows polished and Mary and I washed and brushed with even more than usual vigour in case we should be home for dinner when the Council came.

My mother, rosy with effort, packed us off to school in the morning.

She kissed us on the cheek. "Won't be long before we'll be away from this dump," she promised, looking from right to left up the street. I had never, unlike my older brothers and sisters, regarded our street as a dump.

For me it was a source of entertainment and delightful companionship, so on the way to school I confided in Mary. "We might not like it in the new house, Mary. Rosie Mills says we might even have to go to a different school."

"Rosie Mills is daft," was Mary's only comment.

We rushed home from school at dinnertime to find that a lady from the council had indeed visited our house. My mother sat relaxed in the Windsor chair by the kitchen stove while we ate.

"What did she say, Mum?" Mary asked. "Where is it? When can we move?"

"She didn't say anything. Just looked all over. Even went down to the Trotts. Wrote everything down. She said that there have been nearly a hundred thousand applications this year but that this one will be settled very soon. So it looks as though we are in luck."

My reservations about moving house didn't deter me from spreading the news among my friends in the hope of adding a bit of interest to my personality.

"I expect it'll be miles away," I claimed to Rosie Mills as we chalked up a game of hopscotch on the pavement outside the Shakespeare, "right out in the country."

Throughout the rest of the day, the euphoria remained high. At six o'clock, Miss Godwin came in to congratulate us.

Unmarried with a small child meant that the living in job was a godsend, but Belcher made sure she paid for it. On Sundays she cleaned the flat above the shop and when that was finished, she came to visit her old friend. However, this week she'd managed to get away on Monday and what was more she had procured a pint of winkles from behind Belcher's back.

She raised a wan smile in response to Dad's, "Hallo, how's my gal?"

"Not so pleased about your news as I would like, Alf." Miss Godwin shot my mother a glance, "Depends how far away it is. Don't know what I'd do without you two."

Dad stood up and went over to her, putting his hand on her shoulder. "Don't you worry, gal. We won't be far away. We shan't lose touch. Come on, cheer up! Where's these winkles, then?"

We sat round the table with our bread and butter, each with a pin, and picked our winkles from their shells.

"You'd think it was Sunday," my father remarked. "Visitors AND winkles!"

"It's a special day," replied Mum.

It was weeks before we heard anything more from the council. Mary and I rifled through the dustbin each day in a rescue search for old toys that my mother insisted were broken or finished with. Drawers and cupboards were turned out and Mum was glued to the treadle sewing machine, running up new bedspreads and table covers.

We basked in her good humour and joined eagerly in her frequent rendering of the old music hall songs she sang so beautifully. Even brother John and seventeen-year-old Ginny stopped quarrelling, although John did remark to Ginny that somebody whose name began with P and who worked as a van boy on the lorry that sometimes brought Dad home from work on its way back to the depot was going to be missed. He also suggested in a whisper to me that the house was bound to be haunted – council houses always were – but I didn't believe him.

Then came the day when the envelope, embossed with the London County Council's coat of arms, landed on our doormat at seven o'clock in the morning.

John brought it in and handed it triumphantly to my father. Dad grinned and opened it.

"Mr James," he read aloud, "London County Council Housing Department, 25th September 1928. Sir. We have considered your request to be rehoused under the Local Government Housing Act paragraph 31. While there is no doubt that No. 53 Quebec Road is overcrowded and therefore qualifies for consideration, the London County Council Housing Department has decided that the conditions suffered by your tenants, Mr and Mrs Trott, classify them as top priority nominees for rehousing. We are informing Mr and Mrs Trott of this decision which will be acted upon immediately. This will leave sufficient space at No.53 for your own family and automatically removes your application from the list. Yours etc. J. Smith, Housing Manager, London County Council."

Nobody spoke. Ginny drew in a deep breath. We all looked at my mother. I grabbed my coat from the hook in the hall and made for the front door.

"Where do you think you're going?" thundered my father.

"Out," I said.

16

Herrings at the Slipper Bath

It was Saturday afternoon. Children's pictures were over and so was dinner. Everyone was at home: my father in the big Windsor chair by the kitchen stove, waiting for the football on the radio; my mother busy at one end of the table making the fruit cake for Sunday tea; Mary and I at the other end, cutting squares of newspaper to be strung up in the lavatory outside.

Ginny was spending the whole afternoon as usual in our bedroom. Titivating herself up, as we called it. Saturday night was her dancing night at Streatham Locarno.

"Somebody ought to do something about it, anyway," said my mother, continuing her story about Miss Godwin and Belcher. "He's knocking her about still. He won't let her out and if I stop at the shop to talk to her she's scared stiff he'll come out and start a row."

My father took the pipe from his mouth. "I've told you before, Nell. It's none of your business. You've had it out with him and it's only made it worse. Leave it be."

My brother came in from the garden, a fishing rod in his hand. "Belcher wants a good hiding," he pronounced. "Him and his fancy woman."

My father shot a glance at John's slim five-foot-four torso.

"Who's going to do it, son?" my mother intervened. "Off you go. The fishes will all be in bed if you don't hurry."

She set the cake tin down on the table and gave him an affectionate pat on the shoulder.

Thrusting his arms into his jacket, he left us without another word.

Mary pushed a meat skewer through a neat wad of squared newspaper and threaded a length of string through it. "Sulking again?" There was a note of satisfaction in her voice.

My mother still had Miss Godwin on her mind, however. "Take your pinny off and go up to the shop. I've got that little jumper for Jenny. Take it up there and don't let him see you."

I rose from the table with a show of great reluctance. "Do I have to? It's miles."

Nobody bothered to answer, and I waited for Mum to wrap up the little garment in brown paper.

Out in the street, I started on the rounding-up that usually preceded what was considered a lengthy errand and I had soon collected Rosie,

Bella and Syd. Doughnut was just coming out of his front door on his way to the Slipper Baths and as it was on his way he joined us.

We envied Doughnut. My mother insisted on our taking our weekly baths at home. The big zinc bath would be taken down from the wall in the yard and carried into the scullery in the summer and the kitchen in the winter. Dad would help Mum to fill it with hot water from the copper. As the youngest, I would go in first and Mary next. John no longer participated in the ritual and was allowed the Slipper Baths and so was Dad, but my mother waited until we were all in bed and, replenishing the hot water, would bathe in private while we sat up in bed in our clean nighties, our Sunday clothes laid out on a chair, and waited for Mum to come in to say goodnight.

Doughnut was the only one of our playmates to experience the Municipal Slipper Baths. Bella said she had been once but we didn't believe her. As for Rosie and Syd, a bath of any sort would have been a new experience, unless you can count the dip they had when they visited the swimming pool with the school.

Doughnut was to meet his big cousin outside the Baths. We all knew Jim who, with his round, pasty face and clothes too tight for his pudginess, looked like a larger version of Doughnut himself. Jim was considered 'a shilling short of a quid' in our circles and his presence at the Baths was necessary because Doughnut was too young to be allowed in alone.

We straggled through the familiar streets, listening to Doughnut's enthusiastic description of Saturday at the Slipper Baths.

"It costs threepence each, kids and all, and for that you get a room with a great big bath in it. When you are undressed you yell out the number of your room and the bloke sends the water through the taps and fills it up. If you want more hot or more cold you just shout, 'More cold for Number 3', or 'More hot', whichever you want."

"Is it big enough to swim in? Syd did breast-stroke gestures, running round in a circle.

"Course!"

"You can't swim though," said Rosie.

"I know, but I would if I could!"

We continued on our way under the railway arch, whooping echoes and thinking about the big bath and the hot water coming out of a tap.

Bill Belcher's fish shop stood at the end of a row of shops past the railway arch. Each of the shops in the row came in for some attention. My favourite was the shop that sold stationery, among other things. A dusty jumble of erasers, pencils, notebooks and paintbrushes were on display in the window, each item an object of fascination. We spent long minutes gazing at them before Syd pulled us by our coats into the greengrocer's next door. He stood in front of the display of apples, his shorts several sizes too big, reaching to his calves; tattered jersey tight round his chest; bony chin lifted in a gesture of cheeky defiance. "Got any specks, mister?"

"Clear off!" said the greengrocer.

We turned and ran out of the shop and skipped along the pavement, screaming with laughter.

We stopped at the cobbler's, watching the shoemaker in the window take the nails from his mouth and knock them at precise intervals round the sole of a boot that fitted over the last. We put our heads through the open door to breathe in the strong, leathery smell and to take a good look at the little man in his long canvas apron making a *tap-tap* rhythm with his light hammer.

Best of all was Woody's. Woody didn't operate from a shop but from a sort of shed that spanned an alleyway between the shoemakers and Belcher's. There was a corrugated roof to it and a makeshift door which stood open to the street. Woody was an elderly man who in the summer used the shed as a store for old bicycles which he hired out for twopence an hour. In the winter he spent his days chopping wood into threepenny bundles of kindling and tying them with string. In a district which was as devoid of trees as the Sahara desert he probably did quite well.

Dressed in a big black overcoat and cap and muffler, Woody sat cross-legged in the middle of a mountain of wood chips. He was an amiable old man who was ready to invite us in to sit with him and listen to his stories.

This time we crowded into the little space,

pleased to get out of the late afternoon chill.

"Come on, sit down," invited Woody, "mind you don't get splinters in your bums."

Bella, who was underclad in a yellow party dress chosen from the ample store of her father's rag shop and covered by a skimpy cardigan, sat as near to Woody as she could.

"I'm cold as ice," she complained.

"That reminds me," said Woody, not pausing in his chopping, "did I ever tell you about the time when they roasted an ox on the Thames? The ice was so thick it didn't melt for days after."

"Did you see it, Woody? Did you get some ox?"

"What did it taste like, Woody?"

"Tough. Tough as old boots. Well it would be, wouldn't it? They say 'strong as an ox', don't they? Probably been pulling a couple of tons around all its life. All muscle. Still, you should have seen the lanterns and the crowds and the people skating, and the hot chestnuts and the hot spuds. My father used to let out skates for hire in those days. He did a roaring trade."

The afternoon was growing dark and I suddenly remembered that I was on an errand to the fish shop. "Come on!" I urged. "The shop'll be shut!"

Bill Belcher's shop also stood open to the pavement. Miss Godwin, in a long hessian apron and a pair of shabby boots, was serving a customer. She looked startled when she saw us and looked over her shoulder to the back of the shop. I thrust the parcel into her hand and she quickly put it under the slab. As I turned to leave, she reached to the slab and picked up two fresh herrings, wrapped them in a sheet of newspaper, and gave them to me. "Quick. Off you go. They're for your father's tea."

A roar came from the back of the shop. Belcher came rushing towards us his face red with fury.

Miss Godwin shrank back against the counter, her arms tight across her chest, head down. A wooden box came crashing off the slab as Belcher charged towards us.

"I've told you before. Keep away from my shop. She's not to have anything to do with you lot. Go on, clear off!"

I collided with Rosie as I turned in my haste to get away, hiding the herrings against my chest. We flew down the street, all arms and legs until at last our fright subsided into helpless giggles.

"'Ere," said Doughnut, grabbing Rosie by her dress, "I'm supposed to meet our Jimmy at the Baths. I bet I'm late."

We stopped in our tracks and made our way towards the Baths with some purpose. The damp paper round the fish was disintegrating against my chest and I threw it away. One of the herrings slipped from my arms and Syd pounced on it. Whooping with joy he started slapping it round Bella's legs, chasing her along the pavement. Rosie followed suit and before I could stop her she had the other one, whirling it round her head by its tail.

"Stop it!" I wailed. "They're for my Dad's tea. I'll get in a row."

I ran backwards and forwards in a vain attempt to retrieve the fish. Syd, several inches taller than me, thrust his fish against my face and squeezed the gills. The mouth opened and closed.

"'Ere y'ar. 'E's talking to yer. 'E don't want ter be ate. Do you, fishy?"

Rosie dragged Syd round by his coat.

"Let them 'ave a little talk together, Syd."

She manipulated the gills on her herring and Syd and she performed a fishy pantomime while I jumped up to try to reach them.

Passers-by gave them amused glances and I appealed to Doughnut, the tallest of us all, to get the fish back. Doughnut, not usually the most resourceful of our bunch, after some hesitation responded. He crept up behind Syd and Rosie and with both hands took the herrings from them and thrust them up his jersey. Then off he ran up the street towards the Baths clutching his arms to his chest.

We chased after him and reached the Slipper Baths just in time to see him and Jimmy racing up the green marble steps that led to the entrance. We followed and, as Doughnut and Jimmy disappeared inside, we were stopped by a man in a short white jacket.

"Go on kids, hop it!" he ordered.

"That boy's got my fishes," I protested. He gave me a gentle shove and we found ourselves at the bottom of the steps.

We lingered on the pavement outside the Baths. Doughnut and Jimmy didn't emerge from the big mahogany doors and Syd and the others decided it was time to go home. I wandered disconsolately after them aiming to stop at the fish shop with a faint hope of confessing all to Miss Godwin and getting another two herrings.

If Belcher's not there, I thought to myself, *I know our lovely Miss G will do this for me.*

But Belcher's was closed. The shutters were up on the shop. Woody's ramshackle door was fastened and the light in the cobbler's window was out.

It was dark before I reached home, full of guilt but determined to say nothing about the fish and hoping that my mother's difficulty in contacting Miss G would save the day. Dad had had his tea and so had we. John was home from his fishing and the sight of the proudly displayed roach lying on a plate on the dresser was beginning to get me down.

Ginny came down dressed to go out in a yellow satin dance dress under her coat and little high-heeled sandals.

"Mind you," said Mum as Ginny left, "ten o'clock, and no later."

I sat on my stool by the fire, opposite Dad's chair, my back to the roach and half-contemplating confession.

There was a slight sound from the front door. A soft plop and then another. Mary opened the kitchen door that led to the passage. There on the front doormat lay two herrings, one tailless and both looking very much the worse for wear.

It was two days before I saw Doughnut again. He was walking back from the Junction holding Jimmy's hand.

The return of the herrings through the letter box had left me no alternative but to confess all. To my surprise and relief, the revelation resulted in peals of laughter from Mum and Dad and some good-natured teasing from John and Mary.

I was, however, instructed to find out in detail what had happened to Doughnut and Jimmy and the two fresh herrings inside the Slipper Baths with the steaming hot water all coming out of the tap and the formidable attendants with their white coats and linen towels. I accosted Doughnut and Jimmy and asked them.

Doughnut grinned. "I put 'em down Jimmy's Wellingtons, then we forgot and Jimmy walked home in 'em. That's how the tail came off. Did your Dad eat 'em?"

17

The Vinegar

It was about this time that Mary left school. She had had her fourteenth birthday in March and so she was allowed to leave at Easter. "I want," she announced, "to learn a trade, like Nina Hines's cousin."

"My father put his *Daily Herald* down. "What trade's that, then?"

"The rag trade, over the river, she works in the East End."

"Sweatshop," said Dad, and resumed his reading.

"I want to." Mary's face was set.

"It's too far." My mother looked worried; altercations with Mary were becoming frequent and fraught.

"Look," she was conciliatory, "I know all about Nina's cousin's job, love. It's an apprenticeship, isn't it? She only gets 3/6d a week, and you have to buy all your own stuff: scissors, pipe clay, cottons, soap, the lot. She starts at eight in the morning and finishes at six. You'd have to go miles away, it's over the water. You'd never manage it. And your fares, too."

"I could get a bike."

My brother John called out from the scullery where he was cleaning his boots, "Don't be daft!"

Mary turned round on him. "You can mind your own business. I'd want to be something better than a van boy, anyway!"

"That's enough," murmured my father, continuing to read.

"What do you think, Alf? She can't, can she?"

Dad looked up. "It's up to her." He put his paper down and rose from the chair. "I'm going over the road for a pint. See you presently."

I made to leave with him but my mother called me back.

"I want you to run an errand. Get me a bottle of vinegar from Welman's. Here's thruppence. You can keep the farthing change."

Welman's was at the corner of the street and the sweet shop was a few hundred yards along, on the opposite side of the road. I decided to spend the farthing first, being a pessimist.

There were several of my friends playing in front of the house.

"Where're yer going?" asked Rosie Mills as I started to walk towards the sweetshop.

"Over the sweetshop... coming?"

They all came, of course. It was a matter of principle that if anyone in the group had something to spend, each member had a right to entry. Mr D allowed only bona fide customers inside, but nothing prevented them being accompanied by their friends.

So there were seven of us milling around the little shop.

"What yer going to get?" asked Syd. "How much yer got?"

"I'm going to have a dip, first."

Mr D resignedly took his shoe box from under the counter. The dip cost a farthing and if you were lucky you might pick more than you paid, even as much as twopence. It was a form of gambling that caused as much thrill for us as the Irish Sweepstake did for our elders.

Mr D stood in front of his large glass bottles of sweets arranged on shelves in three tiers. Most, like humbugs, jelly babies and pear drops, were twopence a quarter but arrayed on the front counter were those we preferred. Bright pink sugar shrimps, liquorice sticks, tiger nuts, locust pods and sherbet dabs, each one costing no more than a farthing were those over which we pored in agonies of indecision.

This time, having only drawn a farthing from the box, the front counter was the focus of our attention.

"'Ave a gobstopper," suggested Jackie Rolls, scraping his boots on the front of the counter in an effort to see.

"No, get a liquorice stick," suggested Rosie, "they last longer."

Mr D, meanwhile, looked on in resigned patience, his hands in the pockets of his old grey cardigan, a Woodbine hanging on his lower lip.

"I'll have a sherbet dab," I announced at last.

There was a murmur of congratulations from the gang and we all emerged into the street.

At first we walked in a tight group, each of the others watching me sucking the sherbet-coated lolly stick in sort of vicarious enjoyment, then most of them dispersed, leaving Jackie and me standing outside Welman's.

"Giss a lick."

I dipped the lolly into the sherbet bag and – skilfully avoiding the permanent channel of mucous that was as natural a feature as his nose, and ran to the edge of his upper lip – I thrust it into his mouth.

"Ta," said Jackie. "Giss another lick."

"No," I replied and I went into Welman's.

When I left the shop, the vinegar tightly clutched in my hand, the children had all lined up on the pavement and were about to start a 'Follow My Leader' game. There was some argument between Syd and Rosie contesting the leadership and Rosie won because she could shout louder than Syd, who triumphed in victories requiring subtler tactics. Rosie started down the street, first knocking on Old Mother B's window, which looked over the pavement, causing Mrs B to open her front door and scream at us, an event which yielded us much satisfaction. Rosie ran up and down front doorsteps, calling through the letterboxes, banged on dustbin lids, and quietly followed a young couple immersed so completely in each other that they were unaware of a long queue of children behind them, two by two, gleefully pantomiming their self-absorption.

After a while, Rosie's inspiration petered out and we sat on the kerb, wondering what to do next. I still clutched the vinegar bottle in my hand, ignoring the pleas of the others to 'have a swig'.

Our inactivity was short lived. From the distance we heard what to us was a familiar sound. "It's old 'Enery!" we shouted and eagerly awaited his arrival.

Old 'Enery was so called because the signature tune in his busking repertoire was the famous musical hall tune,

> I'm 'Enery the eighth, I am, I am.
> I'm 'Enery the eighth, I am.
> I got married to the woman next door.
> And she's been married seven times before,
> An' every one was an 'Enery, she wouldn't have a Willy or a Sam
> So I'm 'er eighth old man, I'm 'Enery.
> I'm 'Enery the eighth, I am.

Music, sherbet and friends. What more could a girl want? Just as long as I remembered to get that vinegar safely home to Mum.

18

Scholarship Girl

"She's been chosen!"

Mum put the envelope down on the kitchen table and waved the letter at my father.

"What for?"

"The scholarship. She's passed the scholarship."

He looked up then from the last on which he'd been mending his work boots. "What's that mean, then?"

"Well, it's a better school and that. Not the Grammar. It says here it's a Central School. I've got to take her to see the headmistress on Monday."

My father took the last few nails from between his teeth and knocked them deftly into the leather with a hammer.

There was a long silence whilst he trimmed the leather round the sole of the boot, got off his knees and went to sit at the table. "School Board of London," he read aloud.

My mother and I continued to watch his face. "Do you want her to go?" he said at last.

"I think she should have her chance," said Mum.

He turned and walked towards the scullery door. "Take her, then."

The insurance man was the only one of our acquaintances who could be called a white-collar worker. Although he pedalled his book round on an old bike and often sat by our kitchen fire, either blue with cold or dripping-wet, we felt him to be a step up, so to speak, in the social hierarchy. We saw him as a sort of scout, a kind of infiltrator who had access to mysterious regions peopled by those who had health, wealth, and the amazing gift of knowing the ropes.

So, on Friday evening, after he had entered Mum's weekly shilling in the book, he sat by our fire and read the letter. Mr Braby was in his mid-fifties and, to my mind, the most interesting thing about him was his moustache. It was shiny, black, and waxed at the ends to two needle points. The fascinating part was my father's remark that he wore it like that because he'd been a sergeant in the Great War. It was years before I discovered that it wasn't there to hide a bullet hole or at least a shrapnel scar.

Anyway, he sat there, all tight and smart in his stiff collar, shiny boots and bicycle clips, and agreed with my mother. "She should have her chance." And to me, "You're a clever girl; not many letters about like this, I can tell you."

"It's not the big scholarship, you know," he went on, "it's a sort of half one. You'll be going to that school in Clapham. Learn a trade. Get a good job."

So, on Sunday, my mother finally made up her mind, mended and ironed my very best clothes, gave her grey gabardine a special steaming over the big kettle and hung it to dry in the back yard. I thought somehow that my sisters and brothers, all older than I, seemed to tease me a little less than usual, but I may have imagined it.

On Monday morning, we set off. "All done up like a dog's dinner," said Mum as she stuck her hat pin into the little straw hat with flowers. The hat pin wasn't much help, her bright brown hair always escaped from beneath it. "I'm a right old mess," she'd say, casting an approving glance in the mirror.

The Central School was housed in a building similar to all the other School Board of London establishments. We walked through the corridors with their shiny brown tiles halfway up the walls and the portraits by old masters hanging above. We sat and waited opposite a particularly brown copy of *The Laughing Cavalier* for some minutes before we were shown into the headmistress's study.

Miss Digby was a woman in her early fifties with little bright boot button eyes and short, cropped grey hair. Seated herself behind a desk, she waved my mother to a chair in front of it. She placed me at her side and looked me carefully up and down. "You're small for your age." To me. "Does she eat well?" To my mother. (I ate like a pig.)

"Well, girl, let me tell you about our school. Here, we play hard and we work hard. Here you will learn to be skilled not only in English and arithmetic but in geometry and algebra [*God in Heaven*, I prayed]. You will learn to sew, knit, weave, cook, and later, to type – all to a degree of perfection because that is the slogan of this school – Work to Perfection! So, it's hard work, endeavour and all to reach our goal. The goal of Perfection." She articulated the last word on a quiet downward note, like the Vicar saying "Amen."

There was a reverent pause.

"There you have it, then. What do you think? It's a challenge, isn't it? But, would you prefer a nice juicy steak for your dinner or a tapioca pudding?"

Well, this posed a bit of a problem for me. I'd never eaten a juicy steak, although I liked our steak and kidney puds well enough. The trouble was that tapioca was for me simply food of the gods. I could have happily lived on it! I knew, however, what was expected from me, but in my state, I was hardly capable of answering let alone lying in my teeth. I turned in mute appeal to Mum, who, with a voice husky with tension, coaxed, "Tell Madam, then."

Abandoned, there was only one answer.

"I don't know."

There was a long silence, while she stared at me and I stared at the V neck of her cardigan, broken at last by a gentle tap on the door.

"Enter!" Miss Digby commanded in her man's

voice. The girl who tripped in was about fourteen. Her hair in two silken plaits was the colour of pale gold. She stood opposite us on the other side of the desk in her perfectly pressed gymslip and perfectly laundered white blouse as she confidently placed one cup of tea on the desk in front of the Headmistress.

"Thank you, Gladys."

But this wasn't Gladys! Surely this was Betty Barton, the Captain of the Fourth, who appeared each week in my copy of *School Friend*, in my reveries awake and all my sleeping dreams. The character who never cheated, never lied, who played hockey like an angel. The champion of the right, and ruthless enemy of the wrong. I shrivelled into a reception class infant.

"Gladys is one of our very best pupils. An example to all. She is Captain of her House and her excellent work has taken her to the very top of her year."

I took a further step back into the nursery school.

"Thank you, Gladys. You may go."

Betty Barton turned gracefully towards the door. "Wait, just a minute. Show the new girl your girdle."

Most gymslip girdles I had come across were factory-woven, in plain navy blue; not many children of my acquaintance possessed one anyway, but Gladys's was woven in a rainbow of colours. Blue, red, yellow and green hung in a perfectly arranged circle around her neat waist.

"There, that is her House girdle. One of the first things you will learn here is to make one for yourself."

The threat of algebra may have put fear into my heart, but the girdle business had planted cold terror, no less, so when Miss Digby dismissed us with, "Bring her back this afternoon, we will show you around the school," it was like coming up from near drowning.

As we walked in silence away from the school, my mother took my hand in hers. After a while, she asked, "Well, what did you think about it?"

My throat could only muster a hoarse whisper, "I didn't like her."

"Neither did I, the old bitch!"

"Do I have to go?"

"No, course not. Here, I'll buy you a comic on the way and you can stay at home this afternoon with your old Mum."

19

The Jockey Suit

It was a day in the half-term holidays and it was raining. Mary was working now and carried a handbag with a powder compact in it and a little swansdown powder puff. I had begun to feel abandoned the very day she started work, the change in her was so sudden. She stopped playing in the street with us from the day she left school and went down to the Labour Exchange with Mum to look for a job. She hardly spoke to me when we were indoors and only occasionally would she revert back to our old dreamy discussions in bed.

I had tried to get round her the night before, waiting for what seemed hours before she turned off the gas and slipped into bed beside me.

"Dad says you saw all those men marching about. Tell us about it."

"They're out of work. Go to sleep."

I was quiet for a while, then, "Do you like Nina Mills?"

That'll fetch her, I thought. She hated Nina's guts. It didn't work though and, frustrated, I tried another tack. "Mum don't know you've got that powder compact, does she?"

This got a response alright.

"You tell her and I'll give you a good hiding."

She turned over then and left me alone with my grief.

In the morning I played in the yard until it started to rain. Indoors, Mum was kneeling beside the grate, the blacklead brush in her hand.

"Why don't you find some old comics to change, love? You've got some in the toy box, haven't you?"

I rummaged around the toy box in the cupboard under the dresser. There were two *Funny Wonders*, some old *Film Funs* and a *Comic Cuts*, only last week's.

"Put your coat on!" shouted Mum as I ran out of the front door.

The Rollsies lived nearest, just across the road, but Syd and the other Rolls children never, as far as I knew, bought any comics. I thought I'd have a try and kicked at the knockerless front door until Dolly came clumping along the bare boards of the passage in her boys' boots.

She looked at the comics in my hand.

"Do you want a real jockey's suit?" she demanded.

I passed over the comics and she disappeared into the kitchen at the end of the passage where old Rollsie kept his stock of second-hand clothes. Baby Billy Rolls stuck a mass of matted curls around the kitchen door and put his tongue out.

When Dolly appeared again at the front door, she had the suit draped over her arm. She held it up.

"Here y'ar," she said, "Don't tell nobody."

The costume was made of the finest silk and shone with newness. There were sharp creases down the sleeves and the leggings gleamed white. Not believing in miracles and terrified that Dolly would change her mind, I scuttled through the rain and across the road into our front passage, my new acquisition rolled in a bundle under my arm. The cap fell to the floor and I put it on. My excitement rose. It was real. It was just... wonderful. I passed my hand over the yellow and green silk of the crown and took it off to finger the soft lining. It fitted lightly over my curls and, pushing them underneath, I crouched down, moving my shoulders and arms in a galloping rhythm, pausing only to caress again the fine silk and to glance once more into the mirror. I slipped into the blouse and leggings. It fitted me almost perfectly. Buttoning the top of the blouse, I stood without moving for a long time, silent and breathless, gazing into the mirror at this real jockey in satiny yellow and green, staring back at me, starry-eyed and smiling.

It was then that my mother came out of the kitchen dressed to go out with the oil cloth shopping bag and her fat purse in her hand. She stood dead still for a moment. I smiled up expectantly when, with a single sweep of her arm, she knocked the cap off my head. She spoke through her teeth. "Where did you get that? You got it from the Rolls, didn't you? Get inside!"

I can't remember Mum ever striking me, but she was as near to doing it then as she ever was. She pushed me into the kitchen. "Take that filthy thing off at once!"

She almost tore it off before she threw it onto a little pile of dirty washing under the sink.

"It's not dirty," I protested through my tears, "It's clean. It's nearly new."

My mother's face, red with anger, came closer to mine.

"Nothing's clean from over there," she shouted. "You could get lice and fleas and sores from it. Do you hear me?"

I nodded. My throat dry. She stood looking at me, breathing fast, then closed the kitchen door, her anger subsiding. Her shoulders drooped.

"Hold your noise, now. Come on. You can come shopping with me."

We walked to the high street in silence. After a while, she took my hand.

The rain had stopped and it was becoming dark. The naphtha gas flares on the stalls were already alight, reflecting on the wet pavements and the dripping shop windows. I stood still, silent while my mother bought a pennyworth of pot herbs from the vegetable stall and some meat from the butcher's. In spite of everything: the bustle and noise from the market stalls; the colourful fruit displays and the delicious aroma of pease pudding and faggots being cooked at the butchers, I was not cheered up.

The smell coming from the far end of the market was less enticing but still exciting because it was from the cats' meat shop and that meant coloured comics. Great haunches of horse flesh, covered in flies, hung outside the open shop. The more fastidious customers gave their orders with their handkerchiefs to their noses and their eyes half closed. Today my mother bought two pennyworth, sliced from a bleeding haunch that almost covered the counter while I stood outside, retching. There was a pile of American comics in a wooden box on the floor among the sawdust and I saw my mother pass a coin to the man behind the counter and stoop to pick some up. She thrust them into her shopping bag. I knew they would be damp because they always were, not with contamination from the horseflesh – they were new and clean – but for some mysterious reason which we were never able to discover.

Apart from murmuring, "We'll drop in to see Miss Godwin on the way, duck," my mother didn't speak on the way home.

However, after standing in the open shop talking to Miss Godwin in an undertone and pressing a sixpence into her hand for little Jenny, Mum seemed to cheer up. "You can have Jenny to look after tomorrow, love. If it don't rain you can take her to the rec."

As we left, Bill Belcher came from the back with water in an enamel bucket and threw it over the tub of wriggling live eels.

After tea that evening, my mother spent some time at the sink in the scullery and by the time I had got through the comics, it was time for bed.

As usual, I waited for Mary to get into bed before I slept. I made no attempt to make her respond to me but lay quietly. In the end, as she was about to turn off the gas, she stood gazing down at me.

"What's up with you? You're quiet for a change. You been crying?"

"Mum wouldn't let me have my jockey suit!" It came out in a sort of squeak.

"Oh, is that all? You shouldn't have put it on. You know she washes everything she gets from Rollsie. Never mind. Here, move over and I'll tell you what I did at work today."

The next day I went to fetch Jenny. Miss Godwin hustled her out to me glancing fearfully over her shoulder and whispering to me to get off quickly. The day was fine and Dolly, Syd and Rosie Mills trekked to the recreation ground with us.

When Jenny and I returned home we found the kitchen empty and I could hear my mother in the yard talking over the fence to our next-door neighbour. There was a fire in the kitchen stove and over the big fireguard hung the yellow and green jockey outfit. I picked it off and held it against me. Somehow, all the glamour had come out in the wash.

20

Growing Up –

the Challenge

It must have been about eleven o'clock and we were all ready for bed when the knock came to the door. Two *rat-a-tat-tats* that sent us all out of our skins. My mother was already halfway up the stairs and Dad was performing his regular chore of sweeping the kitchen floor – he did this as a signal that it was time for bed, making us lift up our feet and move our chairs, even when our friends were around. We hated it.

He put the broom down and made for the front door while we stood and waited and my mother paused on the stairs. "It's someone for you. Funny bloody time to come knocking at people's doors, innit? You'd better go and see what he wants."

A young man about my own age dressed in a shabby navy-blue suit stood on the doorstep with a sheaf of newspapers under his arm. He made no preliminary greeting whatsoever.

"Did you fill in a form out of Challenge asking to join the Young Communist League?"

"Yes, that's right."

"We meet every Monday, half past seven in the cafe opposite the station. Go through the cafe and we are upstairs... You will come, won't you?"

He turned to go. At the bottom of the steps he turned round and looked at me for a few seconds. "Don't forget. Half past seven, Monday."

They were all waiting in the kitchen, Mum at the bottom of the stairs. "Who was it?"

Dad had picked the broom up and was leaning on it.

John grinned. "New boyfriend? Must be keen."

"No," I replied, "I've joined the Young Communist League. He's one of them."

They all looked mystified.

"What for?" Mum said as she came into the room.

"Because they're right, aren't they? You know they are."

"I don't know anything of the sort. Who got you into it? First it's the Peace Pledge thing, now it's this." She might have been thinking of the time I'd signed the Toc H life-long Temperance Pledge, aged seven, causing Dad to remark dryly, "That'll save us a fortune in booze money over the years."

Mum sat down on a chair and took off her shoes. "Anyway, I'm ready for bed, do you lot mean to stay up all night?"

The mystification that had greeted the first announcement had turned into hostility and my heart sank as I felt its coldness. They seemed all to speak together.

Ginny laughed. "You don't know anything yet. You want to grow up."

"You're just showing off," Mary sneered.

Brother John was kinder. "Think it over, littl'un. You're on the wrong track."

My father started sweeping again. "Clear off to bed, all of you and let me finish this floor. I've got work tomorrow."

"Mary," I pleaded as we lay in bed together, "people have got to do something, you know, about wars and poor people and everything. And now the blackshirts, the Fascists are even bombing people in Spain. Not just soldiers, but women and children in cities. Don't you think that's terrible? We've all got to get together and organise ourselves to stop it."

"You can't even organise yourself to clear up your mess in this bedroom; anyway, you're barmy," said Mary and turned her back to me. "Stop talking, and go to sleep."

Seven o'clock on Monday evening, I went upstairs to get ready to go to the meeting. My brother followed me out of the kitchen and stood outside the door of the bedroom. I came out onto the landing.

"Are you going?" he asked.

"Course. Look, it was you who kept on about the terrible war. About how awful it was in the trenches for the soldiers. How ordinary people didn't want war, only the governments. That's what started me in the Peace Pledge Movement in the first place."

He shrugged his shoulders. "There's nothing you can do about it. You're just wasting your time on a lot of crackpots."

He called up as he reached the bottom of the stairs, "They've got *Elephant Boy* at the pictures this week. Wanna come Friday?"

My spirits soared. It wasn't an invitation I often received. "Ooh yes. Not half."

There were about a dozen young people sitting on bentwood back chairs in the cafe. The youth who had called on me the week before was seated beside another at a table in front of them. There were two other girls there, one holding the hand of a handsome-looking youngster in a torn shirt and flannel bags with a rent that showed his knee. It seemed that the first young man was called Stan and he was the Branch Secretary. His companion was the Chairman, whose name was Alec.

Stan was as taciturn as he had been at our first meeting, impatient and unsmiling throughout. Alec, dark and somewhat plump, sat leaning back in his chair, relaxed and cheerful.

Procedure was formal. Minutes were read, seconded and passed, familiar to me because of the Trades Union at work and my membership of the local Trades Council. Alec introduced me. I was, he said, a new 'Comrade' and he hoped I would be willing to do everything I could to help build the branch and further the struggle for socialism. Halfway through Alec's welcoming speech, Stan butted in to ask me whether I would be willing to do something right away.

"Certainly," I replied, and he pointed to a Stack of the Young Communist newspaper *Challenge*; a foot-and-a-half thick, which stood on a chair by the table. "We need a *Challenge* organiser, Comrade, would you do it?"

I glowed with pride. Here was this organisation with a secretary and a chairman, engaged in what I believed to be the most vital and crucial work, trusting me with what Stan had said was one of the most important tasks in the branch. I eagerly agreed and, after standing with the others, fist in air la-la-ing the words of *The Internationale*, I found myself in the street with what at first felt like half-a-hundred tons of newsprint under my arm. I walked towards home with fragments of *The Internationale* ringing in my ears:

> Arise ye starvelings from your slumbers.
> Arise you criminals of want.
> For freedom in revolt now thunders...
> We'll change forthwith the old conditions ...

I must learn all of it, I resolved as I sailed along the high street with my feet a foot off the ground, the papers now feeling no heavier than a handful of feathers.

Alec caught me up. "Here, I'll help you carry the papers," he offered.

"Thanks. I hope I can do the job. I've never done anything like it before," I ventured timidly.

"Don't worry about that, mate. Nobody else wants the job, anyway. Old Stan knew you'd take it. Artful sod, excuse my language. Hey, it's getting a bit foggy." He peered around in the gathering gloom. "I go past your place. I'll come with you."

We fumbled our way along the street and I giggled when, bumping into a lamppost Alec, in delightful parody, touched his forehead, bowed low, and murmured, "Sorry, comrade."

We stood for half an hour outside my house, the pile of papers sitting on the doorstep.

"You mustn't take Stan too seriously. He is a wonderful organiser. I'm sure he'll be a great leader one of these days. I just can't help taking the Micky. He never laughs. When you've been in the League a while and got to know us, you'll find out what a good lot they all are. We believe in sharing, that's our reason for belonging and we all act like it between ourselves. One day the whole world will share everything. I truly believe that... so ends the sermon. I'll see you Friday."

Friday? That was my day to see *Elephant Boy* with John! This would be only the first of many such clashes.

Afterword

Battersea and Family in the 1920s

In 1925 in the Metropolitan Borough of Battersea, it was no longer 'considered advisable' to issue closing orders on insanitary dwellings because of the acute shortage of housing. There were two families and a lodger living in Joyce's house then, sharing one tap and an outdoor toilet. A family of ten living in the basement died slowly, one by one, of TB of the bowel[3]. Little surprise then that Joyce identified with the underdog. Battersea, when Joyce lived there, was characterised by overcrowded, privately rented Victorian housing, often with a basement (or 'area' as it was known) and occupied by multiple families. It was a low lying, often damp, area of London, south of the River Thames, and slum clearance by the Borough Council,

---

[3] In the mid-1920s there were nearly 25,000 'working class' dwellings in Battersea, 3,289 of which were not 'reasonably fit' for habitation. In 1925 there were official inspection reports of Insanitary Houses in Meyrick Road and Lavender Terrace, both streets where Joyce's family lived. Infant mortality was 58.4 per 1,000 (it's 3.337 in 2023) and 116 out every 1,000 deaths were due to TB. The average life expectancy for men was 56 (59 for women) - it's 79 and 83 respectively now.

which began to replace the worst slums with three-room tenements at a shilling a week in 1925, was extremely slow. By the 1930s, the whole area was scheduled for housing reform. The diseases of poverty – mental stress, malnutrition, rickets, dangerous and heavy physical work – were exacerbated by respiratory diseases such as TB; and overcrowding spread infestations, infections and contagious illnesses. Front doors were seldom locked (Joyce said that some families actually burnt their front doors in hard times, but this may be an apocryphal tale); keys cost money and there was little to steal. As the story A *Moving Experience* in this collection shows, parents often longed for rehousing, and nostalgia for the camaraderie of poverty – real or imagined – was perhaps a feature of much later slum clearance into tower blocks in the 1960s.

Of course, Battersea in 1925 also contained thriving businesses, factories, riverside wharves, steam laundries, shops, schools, a few chapels and churches, and many pubs. It was bounded on one side by the massive Clapham Junction railway interchange – where Joyce's Dad Alf worked. Battersea employment tended to be unskilled and badly paid, and many workers travelled from outside the Borough because rents there were considered to be high. Two major employers, Prices Candles and Morgan Crucibles, both employed our family members at times but the biggest employers in the first half of the C20th were the railways, gasworks and power station.

At sixteen (in 1936), Joyce sneaked out to join the heaving crowds defying the fascist Moseley's Blackshirts in Cable Street in the largely Jewish East End garment sector, where she met and joined the Young Communist League. Later, her apparently apolitical Dad said laconically to her one evening after yet another meeting, "The rozzers was round here asking where you were." "Did you tell them, Dad?" she replied in alarm. "What d'you think I am? Course not," he said.

Apolitical but unreflectively class-conscious, her parents couldn't really afford to venerate education: reading a book was tantamount to doing nothing when there were chores to be done. Getting and keeping a job; keeping out of debt; keeping clean (no mean feat in the bug-infested slums) – these were the imperatives. Loyalty to family was the keynote of their morality.

Battersea was heavily bombed during the WWII Blitz and provision of shelters was erratic; some families sheltered in the basement, or in indoor Morrison shelters – you needed a garden for an outdoor Anderson shelter – the Tube was too far away. Members of Joyce's family became volunteer Fire Watchers and Joyce was allocated war work at a munitions factory. Ironically, whereas in better-off areas rationing reduced the nutritional value of people's diet, in Battersea (and other poor places) diets significantly improved, bolstered by subsidised milk for mothers and children and greater consumption of vegetables.

As a mature student, Joyce Challis studied by

correspondence course and then, at college, a BA(Hons) English Literature and PGCE. She became a teacher and then Adult Literacy Tutor in South London, where she is remembered for her passion and commitment.

With thanks to Creative Writing Tutor and author Ivan Jones for so warmly encouraging Joyce to write these stories.

Useful Sources

Information about housing stock:
https://www.ucl.ac.uk/bartlett/architecture/sites/bartlett/files/50.08_north_of_clapham_junction.pdf

Information about health in Battersea 1925:
https://wellcomelibrary.org/moh/report/b18220411/119#?c=0&m=0&s=0&cv=100&z=-2.2532%2C0.7128%2C4.1086%2C1.7202

https://enablelc.org/wp-content/uploads/2019/07/Growing-Up-in-Wartime-Battersea-Summary-of-Project.pdf

https://ardingandhobbs.london/

www.ingramcontent.com/pod-product-compliance
Lightning Source LLC
Chambersburg PA
CBHW030301100526
44590CB00012B/470